CW01370046

Ancient China

An Enthralling Overview of Chinese History, Starting from the Settlement at the Yellow River through the Xia, Shang, Zhou, and Qin Dynasties to the Han Dynasty

© Copyright 2023 - All rights reserved.

The content contained within this book may not be reproduced, duplicated, or transmitted without direct written permission from the author or the publisher.

Under no circumstances will any blame or legal responsibility be held against the publisher, or author, for any damages, reparation, or monetary loss due to the information contained within this book, either directly or indirectly.

Legal Notice:

This book is copyright protected. It is only for personal use. You cannot amend, distribute, sell, use, quote, or paraphrase any part, or the content within this book, without the consent of the author or publisher.

Disclaimer Notice:

Please note the information contained within this document is for educational and entertainment purposes only. All effort has been executed to present accurate, up-to-date, reliable, and complete information. No warranties of any kind are declared or implied. Readers acknowledge that the author is not engaging in the rendering of legal, financial, medical, or professional advice. The content within this book has been derived from various sources. Please consult a licensed professional before attempting any techniques outlined in this book.

By reading this document, the reader agrees that under no circumstances is the author responsible for any losses, direct or indirect, that are incurred as a result of the use of the information contained within this document, including, but not limited to, errors, omissions, or inaccuracies.

Free limited time bonus

Stop for a moment. We have a free bonus set up for you. The problem is this: we forget 90% of everything that we read after 7 days. Crazy fact, right? Here's the solution: we've created a printable, 1-page pdf summary for this book that you're reading now. All you have to do to get your free pdf summary is to go to the following website:

https://livetolearn.lpages.co/enthrallinghistory/

Once you do, it will be intuitive. Enjoy, and thank you!

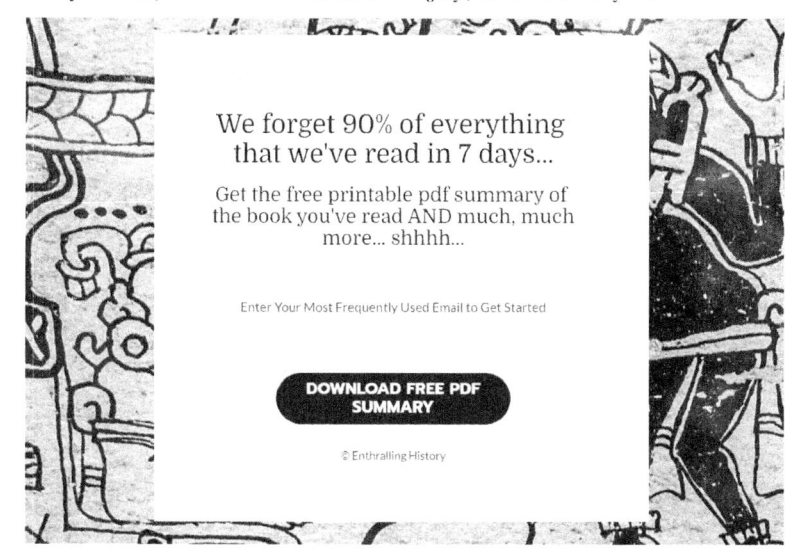

Table of Contents

INTRODUCTION 1
PART ONE: EARLY YELLOW RIVER SETTLEMENTS AND THE XIA DYNASTY 4
CHAPTER 1: PALEOLITHIC CHINA, EARLY YELLOW RIVER, AND YANGTZE RIVER SETTLEMENTS 5
CHAPTER 2: THE XIA DYNASTY: MYTH OR HISTORY? 19
CHAPTER 3: YU THE GREAT 24
PART TWO: THE SHANG DYNASTY (C. 1600-1050 BCE) 27
CHAPTER 4: THE BATTLE OF MINGTIAO 28
CHAPTER 5: CULTURAL AND MILITARY DEVELOPMENTS 32
CHAPTER 6: POLITICS AND RELIGION 37
CHAPTER 7: THE FALL OF THE SHANG DYNASTY 44
PART THREE: THE ZHOU DYNASTY (C. 1050-221 BCE) 47
CHAPTER 8: WESTERN AND EASTERN ZHOU DYNASTIES 48
CHAPTER 9: CULTURAL DEVELOPMENTS 54
CHAPTER 10: FALL OF THE ZHOU DYNASTY 62
PART FOUR: THE QIN DYNASTY (221-206 BCE) 64
CHAPTER 11: RISE OF THE QIN DYNASTY AND QIN SHI HUANGDI 65
CHAPTER 12: THE EXPANSION OF CHINA AND THE FALL OF THE QIN DYNASTY 68
CHAPTER 13: CULTURAL DEVELOPMENTS 71
CHAPTER 14: THE END OF FEUDALISM 75
CHAPTER 15: THE BURNING OF BOOKS AND THE BURYING OF SCHOLARS 77
PART FIVE: THE HAN DYNASTY (206 BCE-220 CE) 80
CHAPTER 16: RISE OF THE HAN DYNASTY 81
CHAPTER 17: WESTERN AND EASTERN HAN DYNASTIES 91
CHAPTER 18: CULTURAL AND MILITARY DEVELOPMENTS 98
CHAPTER 19: THE FALL OF THE HAN DYNASTY 106
CONCLUSION 110
HERE'S ANOTHER BOOK BY ENTHRALLING HISTORY THAT YOU MIGHT LIKE 116
FREE LIMITED TIME BONUS 117
BIBLIOGRAPHY 118

Introduction

We have all witnessed the incredible economic development of China in the last few decades. But this is only a very small fraction of Chinese history. China has the longest continuous cultural development of all modern countries. Yes, the ancient Egyptian civilization is older than the Chinese civilization, but ancient Egypt came under the influence of other religions, which suppressed their older traditions. China, on the other hand, has remained connected to its roots, which span back to the Paleolithic Age (the Old Stone Age) and possibly even further.

It's quite remarkable that Chinese people today can somewhat understand even the oldest inscriptions dating from the period of the Shang dynasty (2nd millennium BCE). This is what we mean by the *continuity* of a culture. Age-old inscriptions found on oracle bones and turtle shells from the Shang dynasty bear Chinese characters similar to those still used today.

Fast forward one millennium, and we're in the period of the famous Confucius (the 6th to 5th centuries BCE), who does not lag behind the great minds of ancient Greece. In fact, Confucius predates a majority of ancient Greek philosophers, apart from the Milesians (Thales, Anaximander, and Anaximenes).

Jumping forward five hundred years, we encounter the great Han dynasty, which is famous for bringing forth the Golden Age of China (today, we might rightfully say the first "Golden Age"). The Han ruled between the 3rd century BCE and the 3rd century CE. They are very much responsible for the modern Han identity of the Chinese. During this period, there was a highly ordered Chinese society with a centralized government, distinct and diverse social classes, and a well-functioning administration.

This book, for the most part, will remain between the prehistoric roots of Chinese culture and the fall of the Han dynasty (covering a period of more than ten thousand years, from the 10th millennium BCE to the 1st millennium CE). It is virtually impossible to write a fairly short yet good book on all of Chinese history, as it is a challenge to do so just for the country's prehistory. But from the Han dynasty onward, so many things happened in China until the ultimate dissolution of the Chinese Empire in the early 20th century under the Qing dynasty. And even after that, there was the ensuing Warlord era, revolutionary chaos, and the victory of the Chinese Communist Party.

History is fractal in nature. When you look a bit more carefully, things start unraveling in all sorts of directions, and you're amazed at their sheer complexity. However, there is a sort of "recency" bias, namely, more recent events tend to be remembered in a more detailed manner. It is for this reason that most people focus on the 20th-century history of China, Mao Zedong, and China's ultimate economic success. But if you look with the right kind of eyes, even far back to prehistoric times, you'll start understanding this fractal nature of (pre)history. And this is exactly what we'll be doing in this book. We'll take distant events, which at first glance seem so minuscule, maybe even nonsignificant, and we'll put them under the microscope to observe how one event grows and divides into numerous other events, establishing unfathomable links between themselves.

By doing this, we'll be able to understand the essence of modern China and how this great culture endured for so many centuries. There were many great cultures throughout history, such as the ancient Greeks, Persians, Romans, and Maya, to name a few. But the Chinese culture is the only one that survived mostly intact. There is something in Chinese culture that allows it to continue existing even though other cultures crumbled under the burden of the sands of time. And to learn what that something is, we have to look back, way back. Maybe we won't be able to find that something. Maybe we'll find out that there are actually many things that make the Chinese culture so special. And maybe, just maybe, we'll learn how to use this knowledge to further improve the world we are living in. In any case, it will be an interesting ride! Sit back, relax, and come with us on a travel through time. Destination: paleolithic China (pre-10,000 BCE).

PART ONE: EARLY YELLOW RIVER SETTLEMENTS AND THE XIA DYNASTY

Chapter 1: Paleolithic China, Early Yellow River, and Yangtze River Settlements

To understand the formation and significance of early Yellow River settlements, we have to juxtapose them with their precursors, the Paleolithic societies in China. It's important to note that we don't exactly know to what extent Paleolithic and Neolithic peoples in China are related, nor do we know to what extent modern Han Chinese are related to people who lived in China thousands of years ago.

Human and human-like fossils from the Paleolithic Age are found throughout the whole of China. The Zhoukoudian cave system, on its own, preserved a wealth of fossils dating from various sub-periods of the Paleolithic Age.[1] This age is by far the longest in the development of humans. The so-called Peking Man who inhabited the Zhoukoudian caves is at least 700,000 years old, possibly even older.[2] The cave system is home to the remains of *Homo erectus*, a species that was perhaps the

---

[1] Chang, Kwang-Chih. "In Search of China's Beginnings: New Light on an Old Civilization: A Golden Age of Archaeology is piecing together a new Chinese prehistory and history that differ in fundamental ways from the traditional story." *American Scientist* 69, no. 2 (1981): 148-160.

[2] A very loose term used to denote human remains found in Zhoukoudian Caves. There are many layers of archaeological findings in these caves, and it is not clear how these layers relate between themselves.

first to start using and constructing simple stone tools. Even though members of *Homo erectus* weren't entirely like modern humans, they walked upright and used tools. In any case, they inhabited Eurasia a long, long time ago. The Peking Man isn't even the oldest fossil remains of human-like primates. The oldest is the Yuanmou Man, which dates back to at least 1.7 million years ago.[3] The Yuanmou Man was also a *Homo erectus*.

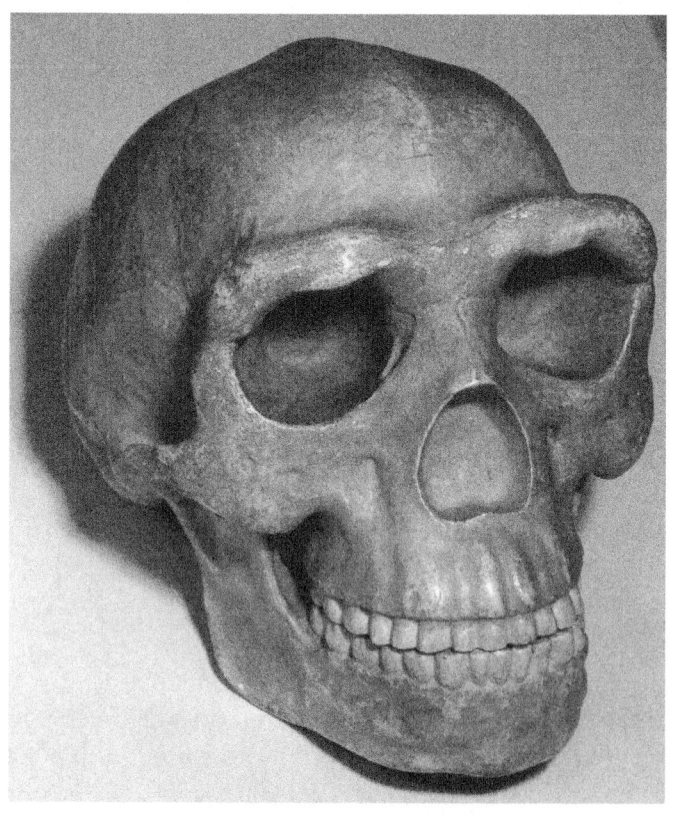

Peking Man skull (reconstruction).
Kevin Walsh; https://creativecommons.org/licenses/by/2.0/.
https://www.flickr.com/photos/86624586@N00/10191736

---

[3] Pu, Li, Chien Fang, Ma Hsing-Hua, Pu Ching-Yu, Hsing Li-Sheng, and Chu Shih-Chiang. "Preliminary study on the age of Yuanmou man by palaeomagnetic technique." *Scientia Sinica* 20, no. 5 (1977): 645-664.

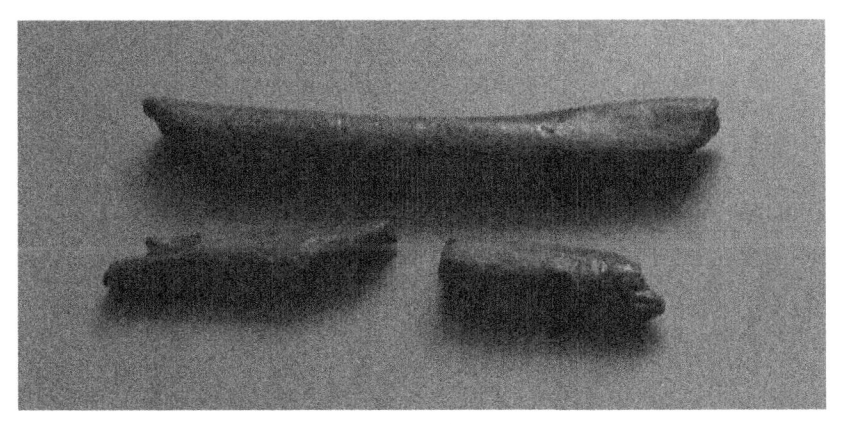

Remains of a human tibia bone, Yuanmou area.

Zhangmoon618, CC BY-SA 4.0 <https://creativecommons.org/licenses/by-sa/4.0>, via Wikimedia Commons; https://commons.wikimedia.org/wiki/File:%E4%BA%91%E5%8D%97%E7%9C%81%E5%8D%9A%E7%89%A9%E9%A6%86-%E6%97%A7%E7%9F%B3%E5%99%A8%E6%97%B6%E4%BB%A3-%E5%85%83%E8%B0%8B-%E5%85%83%E8%B0%8B%E4%BA%BA%E8%83%AB%E9%AA%A8%E5%8C%96%E7%9F%B3.jpg

The oldest inhabitants of China, as was typical for the Paleolithic Age in general, were hunter-gatherers who lived in small communities. They constructed and used stone tools for hunting and other purposes. Apart from that, we don't know much about these "proto-people." It's possible they engaged in cannibalism.[4] However, these people formed communities and probably hunted in organized groups.

Fossils dating back to around thirty-five thousand to thirty thousand years ago provide evidence of a gradual change in Chinese Paleolithic cultures. Stone refinement techniques became more sophisticated, and it is from this period that we obtain the first evidence of arts and symbolic activities, which are an important "marker" of human nature.[5] This gradual movement, which occurred late in the Paleolithic Age, is marked by the rise of *Homo sapiens*. Numerous *Homo sapiens* fossils were unearthed in China, some being 200,000 years old.

The Paleolithic Age is one big mystery in the development of humanity. Drastic cultural progress happened in the Neolithic Age (New Stone Age). Therefore, the evidence for the Neolithic Age is much more

---

[4] Boaz, N., and R. Ciochon. "The scavenging of "Peking Man." *Natural History* 110, no. 2 (2001): 46-51.

[5] Gao, Xing. "Paleolithic cultures in China: uniqueness and divergence." *Current Anthropology* 54, no. S8 (2013): S358-S370.

abundant, as people started using more complex ways to express themselves and their mastery of their surroundings. The Paleolithic Age, on the other hand, is relatively scarce with respect to archaeological findings, so we can only make loose conjectures about how Paleolithic people lived. This is why there are many interpretations of the Paleolithic Age, and many authors have used it in different ways to prove their claims.

For instance, Sigmund Freud believed that way back in prehistory, people's most powerful impulses, sex and aggression, were manifested in much more straightforward ways compared to today.[6] Freud went as far as to claim that the Oedipus complex, which, according to him, exists in an implicit and symbolic form in all of us, was manifested in a much more real way. Because Paleolithic communities were formed around one powerful male who "possessed" all females and was the leader of the group, Freud presumed that other males (e.g., the sons of an alpha male) grew jealous and wanted to get rid of the alpha male. So, they killed their own (real or symbolic) father and ate his flesh in a sort of ritual that bound them together in their guilt.[7] Freud goes as far as to claim that this prehistoric Oedipus complex served as a basis for a less violent society. Those who killed the alpha male were held together with strings of communal guilt, and they gradually learned how to divide power amongst themselves more rationally to avoid internal strife. Due to guilt and fascination with the power of a long-gone alpha male, people were compelled to make a sort of totem, which they venerated. This is how Freud explains an important moment in the early formation of religions.

Whether you believe in this story or not, Freud really did try to understand the psychology of prehistoric people. Though he may have overestimated the importance of the Oedipus complex (both for individual and phylogenetic[8] development), he succeeded in painting a believable prehistoric scene. Prehistoric communities (especially early in the Paleolithic Age) were kept together by sheer necessity, physical

---

[6] Freud, Sigmund. Moses and monotheism. *Leonardo Paolo Lovari*, 2016.

[7] This is another conjecture about the Paleolithic Age, namely the "alpha male" theory. While it's very likely that physical prowess was of the utmost importance back then, we still don't know a lot about the social hierarchy of the Paleolithic Age. In other words, it's possible that early prehistoric communities had a strong male leader, but we don't really know the extent of his power and control over his "subordinates."

[8] Development of a species.

dominance of one (or a handful) of members, and fear. Impulses that we have driven to the unconscious were likely expressed in a more direct manner back then. Language, if it even existed in the Paleolithic Age, was also coarse and probably very different from the languages we speak today. They probably varied even across fairly small areas. It's also due to the relative coarseness of early languages that people had to find other, more direct means to express their desires.

The Paleolithic Age is, thus far, the longest period in the development of humanity. And yet we have to remain content with conjectures, hypotheses, and suppositions when it comes to explaining how people lived in this (very long) period. This early period of the development of humanity will probably forever remain veiled in the mystery of time, and it will always be a period that necessitates a peculiar combination of scientific and artistic types of thinking to be explained.

Early Yellow River and Yangtze River Settlements in the Neolithic Age

A lot of things happened (not only in China but also in Europe and the Middle East) that made the Paleolithic people gradually adopt a different lifestyle. Although the people didn't abandon hunting and foraging, they started learning how to control their sources of life. Namely, they started controlling their two main sources of food, plants and animals, leading to the birth of agriculture and domesticated animals. As is the case with most things that happened in prehistory, we don't really know how this shift happened. There are many possible scenarios of how people discovered they could domesticate wild animals or sow seeds of a plant. Once again, these were probably gradual processes and varied greatly across different geographical locations.

In any case, around ten thousand years ago, the Neolithic Age was well under way in China. There are many markers of the Neolithic cultures, with pottery, large permanent settlements, organized cultivation, and the processing of plants being some of the most important markers.

Nanzhuangtou is perhaps the oldest Neolithic Chinese culture. The Nanzhuangtou culture was situated in China's modern-day northern Hebei province. This culture is around ten thousand years old, perhaps even older, and it gave us the first evidence of millet consumption and cultivation.[9] Members of the Nanzhuangtou also domesticated dogs (one

---

[9] Yang, Xiaoyan, Zhikun Ma, Jun Li, Jincheng Yu, Chris Stevens, and Yijie Zhuang. "Comparing

of the first animals to be domesticated, globally speaking), and they also made and used pottery.[10] Generally speaking, the Nanzhuangtou culture is so different compared to other evidence of human activity from the Paleolithic Age.

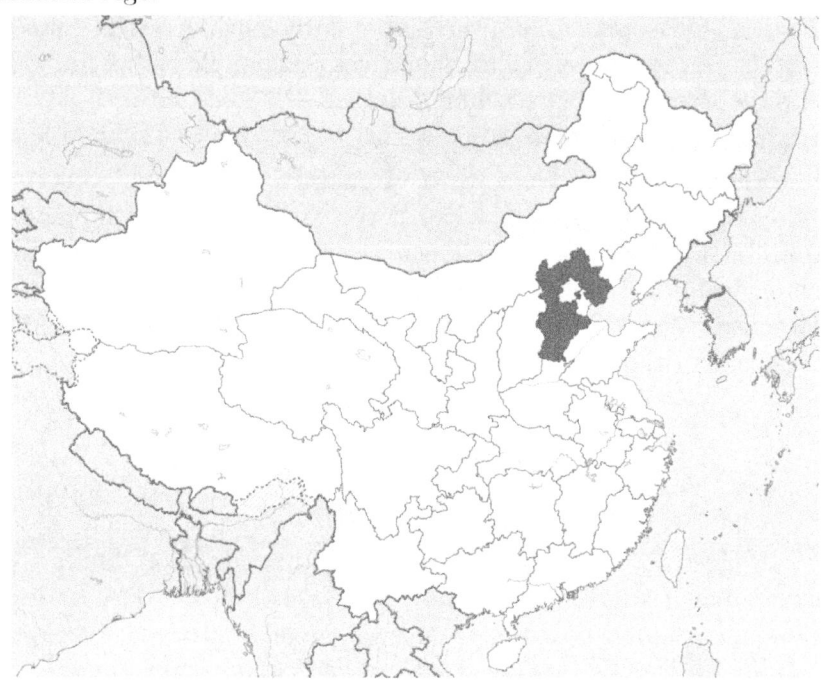

Location of modern-day Hebei province, the location of the Nanzhuangtou culture.
TUBS, CC BY-SA 3.0 <https://creativecommons.org/licenses/by-sa/3.0>, via Wikimedia Commons; https://commons.wikimedia.org/wiki/File:Hebei_in_China_(%2Ball_claims_hatched).svg

With the Peiligang culture (around eight thousand years ago), Chinese agriculture saw an immense developmental step. This culture was situated in modern-day Henan province in the basin of the Yellow River. Members of the Peiligang culture cultivated a wide variety of plants, such as broomcorn and foxtail millet.[11] Agriculture requires careful planning and management of resources. The Peiligang people possibly engaged in

---

subsistence strategies in different landscapes of North China 10,000 years ago." *The Holocene* 25, no. 12 (2015): 1957-1964.

[10] Jing, Yuan. "The origins and development of animal domestication in China." *Chinese Archaeology* 8, no. 1 (2008): 1-7.

[11] Bestel, Sheahan, Yingjian Bao, Hua Zhong, Xingcan Chen, and Li Liu. "Wild plant use and multi-cropping at the early Neolithic Zhuzhai site in the middle Yellow River region, China." *The Holocene* 28, no. 2 (2018): 195-207.

organized tilling of soil and soil improvement, as well as weeding out unnecessary and obnoxious plants that would take nutrients and light from the crops. Irrigation and watering were also basic activities for the Peiligang people. Irrigation and control of the big rivers, such as the Nile or Yellow River, were probably the first large-scale engineering feats of humanity. And while the Egyptians were learning how to control the great power of the Nile, the ancient Chinese were learning how to control their immense rivers, such as the Yellow River and the Yangtze River. The Peiligang people didn't only eat their domestic crops. They also relied heavily on various sorts of nuts and fruits, such as walnuts, hazelnuts, acorns, jujube, plums, and others.

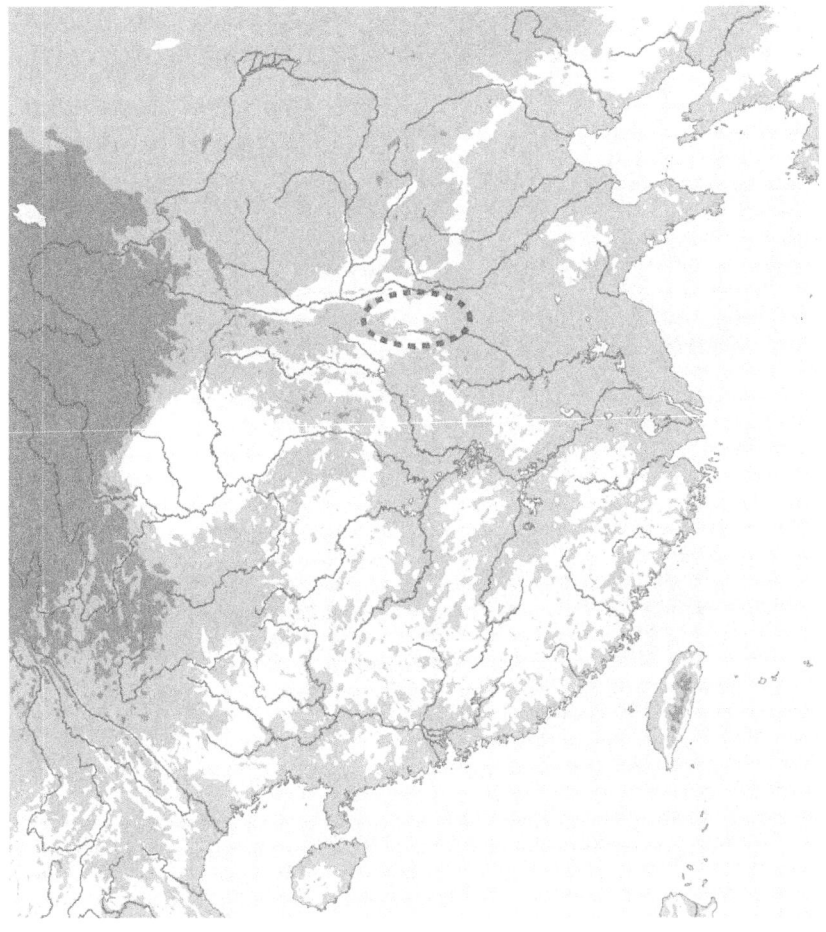

The location of the Peiligang culture in modern-day Henan province in mainland China. *Kanguole, CC BY-SA 4.0 <https://creativecommons.org/licenses/by-sa/4.0>, via Wikimedia Commons; https://commons.wikimedia.org/wiki/File:Peiligang_map.svg*

The Peiligang people were skilled potters. To make pottery, one has to learn how to build a fire that can reach very high temperatures and sustain that heat. People becoming more skilled in controlling fire was another crucial engineering feat of the Neolithic Age. Neolithic people, the Peiligang included, were able to build ovens that could produce and sustain temperatures needed for baking pottery. These were possibly underground ovens, which, thanks to the insulation properties of soil, were crucial in creating good pottery.

Peiligang pottery in Shanghai Museum. This piece has characteristic "ears" and dates from a later period of the Peiligang culture, from the 7th or 6th millennia BCE.
User:Captmondo, CC BY-SA 3.0 <http://creativecommons.org/licenses/by-sa/3.0/>, via Wikimedia Commons; https://commons.wikimedia.org/wiki/File:PeiligangCulture-RedPotWithTwoEars-ShanghaiMuseum-May27-08.jpg

The Peiligang people made all sorts of vessels, tripods, double-handed jars, cups, dishes, bowls, and other things.[12] Their pottery is rarely adorned with works of art, though some have geometrical ornaments as decoration. We also have numerous spades, axes, sickles, and grinding stones dating from this period, which are testaments to the Peiligang culture's technological development and diversity in crafts. Interestingly, the tools of one type seem to have roughly been the same size, which means that sharing craftsmanship knowledge was already standardized to a certain extent in Peiligang culture. It's possible that some people already specialized in making pottery, while others specialized in making stone tools or simply worked as farmers. They also domesticated dogs, pigs, sheep, chickens, and cattle.

Although we don't know much about the social life of the Peiligang people, it is likely they lived in more or less permanent villages and had an elaborate system of religious beliefs. Archaeologists have uncovered numerous sacrificial pits, with domestic animals used as sacrifices. Chickens were often used as sacrificial offerings, especially roosters, which probably means that male chickens had some sort of symbolic value for the Peiligang. Sacrifices were frequent and probably were an important part of everyday life.

The Neolithic Age is sometimes seen as an idyllic period, a period when people lived in harmony with their environment and each other. Remember, they were still in the Stone Age, and though weapons existed in the Stone Age, they weren't as effective as the weapons that would come later. The people weren't as numerous, and there wasn't a pressing need to find new territory, as there was enough land for everyone.

However, it's likely that the Neolithic Age saw a drastic increase in population. People learned how to make and preserve food on their own and weren't as dependent on hazardous searches for food or hunting. Moreover, the Neolithic Age probably saw the first significant accumulation of wealth. And when you have wealth, you also have people who want to obtain it by any means possible. These two factors prove crucial for explaining the period that comes right after the Neolithic Age, the Age of Metal. With more and more people and more and more wealth, the scene was set for a more turbulent and violent age.

---

[12] Guoping, Sun. "Recent research on the Hemudu culture and the Tianluoshan site." *A companion to Chinese archaeology* (2013): 555-573.

The accumulation of wealth allowed for a more intricate separation of classes within society, with some people being wealthier and others less so.

The evidence of Neolithic cultures in the basin of the Yangtze River stems back to at least ten thousand years ago.[13] The earliest evidence of rice cultivation in the Lower Yangtze comes from the Shangshan culture (ten thousand years), in the form of stone tools, such as scrapers and burins (stone flakes with sharp tips). There were also sharp tools that were used to harvest plants. The ingenious methodology of archaeologists makes it possible to test if a stone tool was used for harvesting plants. In the case of the Shangshan, archaeologists have found numerous stone tools with acute edges. Plants leave residue on stone tools (and to prove just how and to what extent, modern archaeologists have to make real-life experiments) and wear-and-tear marks (just what kind of marks is also something we learn through modern experiments).

The Shangshan people were the first sedentary group of people in the region of the Lower Yangtze; in other words, they weren't nomads but formed permanent villages. One such Shangshan village is around thirty thousand square meters in size, with designated spaces for living, storage, burials, and waste disposal. But this was just the start of agriculture. and We'll have to wait another few thousand years to pass before we see "fully fledged" agriculture and civilization in the Yangtze River Basin.

The Liangzhu culture (4,300 to 5,300 years ago) was the most technologically advanced of all the Neolithic cultures in the Lower Yangtze region before the great flood. Yes, even back then, people had problems with climate change. It seems that around 4,300 years ago, people in China experienced great climate perturbations ending in catastrophic floods.[14] They brought an end to the well-developed Liangzhu culture, which had its own capital city that was defended by walls and adorned with palaces. The Liangzhu people were probably well known in their age for their jade industry (we have some beautiful

---

[13] Wang, Jiajing, Jiangping Zhu, Dongrong Lei, and Leping Jiang. "New evidence for rice harvesting in the early Neolithic Lower Yangtze River, China." *Plos one* 17, no. 12 (2022): e0278200.

[14] Zhang, Haiwei, Hai Cheng, Ashish Sinha, Christoph Spötl, Yanjun Cai, Bin Liu, Gayatri Kathayat et al. "Collapse of the Liangzhu and other Neolithic cultures in the lower Yangtze region in response to climate change." *Science Advances* 7, no. 48 (2021): eabi9275.

evidence of their craft) and a good water-management system.

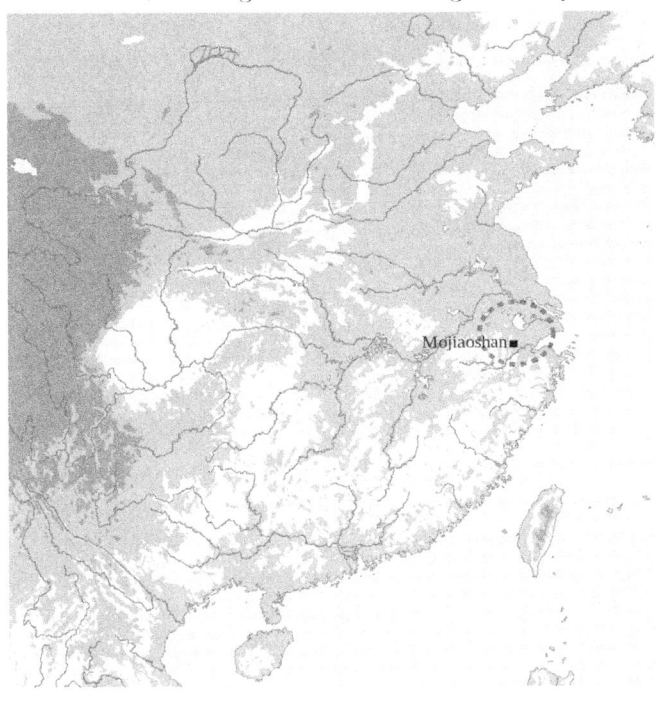

The location of the Liangzhu culture in the Lower Yangtze, modern-day Zhejiang province. Kanguole, CC BY-SA 4.0 <https://creativecommons.org/licenses/by-sa/4.0>, via Wikimedia Commons; https://commons.wikimedia.org/wiki/File:Liangzhu_map.svg

With Liangzhu, we're already in a world more similar to the one we're living in today. If we skip back "just" ten thousand years before, we would be back in the Paleolithic Age, which is much stranger and more distant to humans today. But in the Liangzhu culture, we encounter the makings of the modern age, such as elaborate social stratification, complex death and burial rituals, and more. In fact, social stratification and burials are closely related; by exploring the cemeteries of the Liangzhu, we are able to make inferences about their social structure.

The Liangzhu people were very careful about their cemeteries. They were always located on higher ground, and if there wasn't such a location nearby, the Liangzhu would build a mound or a hillock for the purpose of burials. Their social stratification was preserved even in death. The elites were placed at the top of the hillock, and less elite members went to the bottom.[15] Most evidence relating to the Liangzhu comes from

---

[15] Ling, Qin. "The Liangzhu culture." *A companion to Chinese archaeology* (2013): 574-596.

cemeteries since these were situated on higher grounds, making them easier to find them. Villages that were placed on lower ground became covered by layers of sediment. Archaeologists found numerous everyday objects in burial sites, such as stone axes, jade objects, and pottery. Ceramic pots, tripods, stemmed dishes, jars, and basins have also been found in abundance. Interestingly, males were buried with stone axes and jade objects, while women were buried with circular and plate ornaments.

One of the ways the Liangzhu expressed wealth was by the number of objects in a burial site. The more things a person could afford to send to the other world, the richer they were. Jade seems to have been a status symbol. The Liangzhu produced jade objects, adorned them, and distributed them. The three main motifs were dragons, humans, and sacred animals and appeared separately on jade objects, perhaps indicating their different meanings in the Liangzhu religion. Similar motifs appeared on Liangzhu pottery. The differences between the jade and pottery representations of, say, dragons can be taken as evidence of craft specialization among the Liangzhu. By analyzing the decoration of jade and pottery objects, archaeologists have concluded that these were decorated by different craftsmen.

A luxurious jade object with intricate ornamental decorations made by Liangzhu craftsmen. Located in the Provincial Museum of Zhejiang.
Zhangzhugang, CC BY-SA 3.0 <https://creativecommons.org/licenses/by-sa/3.0>, via Wikimedia Commons; https://commons.wikimedia.org/wiki/File:Zhejiang_Sheng_Bowuguan_2014.09.28_15-27-39.jpg

Let's briefly turn toward more monumental achievements of the Liangzhu. Near modern-day Hangzhou, remains of a Liangzhu urban center were discovered. The most important discovery in this sense is the long city wall, which enclosed an area of about 290 hectares. The wall was probably around four meters high and had a very solid rock base. This wall is not only a testament to the construction capabilities of the Liangzhu but also to the increasing need to defend wealth. As we've already mentioned, during the Neolithic Age, humans really started to accumulate wealth. While the people had an intricate status differentiation within communities, they also had increasing differences between various groups.

It's possible that war, as we know it today, originated around the time of the Neolithic Age. Indeed, the most important achievements of the Neolithic Age, namely a sedentary lifestyle, the accumulation of wealth, and the emergence of status differentiations within and between groups, can be seen as the prerequisites of organized warfare.[16] It's true that aggression, conflicts, massacres, skirmishes, and things like that existed since the dawn of humanity, but the emergence of organized warfare is probably a newer "invention" dating back to the Neolithic Age. The Neolithic humans were also skilled craftsmen and were able to make increasingly effective weapons. Yes, these weapons were made of stone or wood, so they wouldn't be as effective as weapons made of bronze or iron. The world had to wait for the Age of Metal and the further perfection of the art of warfare before things got really bloody.

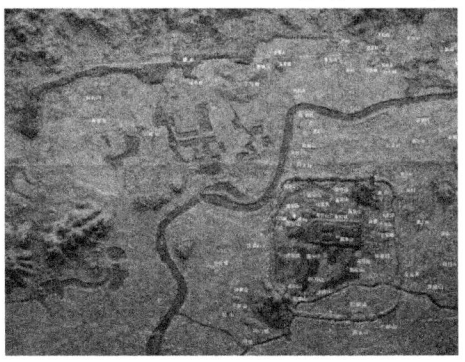

A model of the Liangzhu capital. The bottom right quarter represents the rectangular walled area, with something like a palace or castle in the middle. The walled area itself is surrounded by buildings that would have had various economic purposes.
猫猫的日记本, CC BY-SA 3.0 <https://creativecommons.org/licenses/by-sa/3.0>, via Wikimedia Commons; https://commons.wikimedia.org/wiki/File:Model_of_Liangzhu_Ancient_City_01_2013-10.JPG

---

[16] Runnels, Curtis N., Claire Payne, Noam V. Rifkind, Chantel White, Nicholas P. Wolff, and Steven A. LeBlanc. "Warfare in Neolithic Thessaly: A case study." Hesperia: *The Journal of the American School of Classical Studies at Athens* 78, no. 2 (2009): 165-194.

Let's briefly discuss another great achievement of the Neolithic Age, the one we're still using in more or less the same form today: the invention of alcoholic beverages. Fairly early in Neolithic China, some eight thousand years ago, people started to experiment with alcohol fermentation.[17] All sorts of beverages were made from plants like broomcorn millet, Job's tears (Adlay millet), beans, ginger, rice, lily, yam, and others. The Chinese people used various fermentation techniques, such as cereal malts, moldy grains, and special herbs. One invention was crucial for the discovery of alcohol fermentation: pottery. Special vessels for alcoholic beverages were made in early Neolithic China. Without such vessels, it would have been impossible to preserve any kind of liquid for extended amounts of time. The earliest Chinese alcoholic beverages (and Neolithic alcoholic beverages in general) probably had fairly low alcohol percentages. The world had to wait a bit longer for the emergence of stronger alcoholic beverages until the distillation process was invented. The Neolithic drinks were probably somewhat similar to beer or wine, though, as we've seen in the case of China, many different variations were possible. Moreover, we don't really know what purpose these early drinks served. Scholars hypothesize that alcoholic beverages in Neolithic China probably had medicinal, social, and spiritual uses.

And this is the broad landscape of Neolithic China. It was a marvelous period in the development of humanity. In the space of "only" a few thousand years, the Neolithic Age brought tectonic changes to humanity and propelled China (and others) into the historical period (as in the written age). But before we deal with the first written evidence from China, let's turn to one big mystery that still exists because of the blurred lines between myth and history—the Xia dynasty.

---

[17] Liu, Li, Jiajing Wang, Maureece J. Levin, Nasa Sinnott-Armstrong, Hao Zhao, Yanan Zhao, Jing Shao, Nan Di, and Tian'en Zhang. "The origins of specialized pottery and diverse alcohol fermentation techniques in Early Neolithic China." *Proceedings of the National Academy of Sciences* 116, no. 26 (2019): 12767-12774.

Chapter 2: The Xia Dynasty: Myth or History?

According to an age-old story, the Xia dynasty was an illustrious dynasty that ruled over a prehistoric Bronze Age Chinese culture. Scholars aren't unanimous when it comes to the existence of this dynasty and whether we can establish a connection between the Xia dynasty and one or several Bronze Age cultures of China, which are numerous.[18] First, let's give a little bit of context.

We have jumped from the Neolithic Age straight to the mythical Xia dynasty. The end of the Neolithic Age in China was marked by the invention of copper tools and weapons, which, in general, can be considered the first metal to be crafted into tools by humans.[19] Copper items, such as spearheads, started to emerge in the 3rd millennium BCE (five thousand years ago) in modern-day western China.[20] Copper isn't

---

[18] Thorp, Robert L. "Erlitou and the search for the Xia." *Early China* 16 (1991): 1-38.

[19] There's a reason copper was the first metal to be extracted and crafted by humans. Unlike most other metals, it can be found in a relatively pure form in nature. In order to use other types of metals, more elaborate extraction methods had to be put into place. Moreover, copper has a lower melting point compared to iron or alloys like steel. Interestingly, bronze, which was a metal invented immediately after copper, has a similar melting point to copper. Thus, the furnaces had to evolve correspondingly.

[20] Bunker, Emma C. "The Beginning of Metallurgy in Ancient China" *Web Archive*. Available at: https://web.archive.org/web/20070206143502/http:/exhibits.denverartmuseum.org/asianart/articles/metalwork/art_li_mat.html

that sturdy, and people soon found a way to make it more durable. They added tin, creating bronze. This was a period of experimenting with mixing different metals and observing the outcome. The Chinese quickly became skilled metal craftsmen, and in Chinese classical literature, we have evidence of how people back then were aware of how mixing metals in different proportions had differing outcomes.

Around four thousand years ago in prehistoric China, numerous Bronze Age cultures emerged, among them the famous Erlitou culture. The Erlitou people lived in the basin of the Yellow River, modern-day Henan province. Needless to say, they mastered agriculture and had large permanent settlements and an urban center. They were also skilled in making various bronze objects, such as wine vessels. The remains of a palace were also found, testifying to the existence of an Erlitou elite. The palace was surrounded by a sturdy wall built by compressing the earth and other materials together. Here's an expert description of this building:

"The compound stood on a broad pounded earth platform ... Walls enclosed this area, but little except their footings survives. Roofed galleries were probably created by the addition of parallel rows of columns both inside and outside the walls. At the center of the south wall was a large opening in the wall measuring 34 m across interpreted as a gate, but this portion of the site is so poorly preserved that little about the appearance of this gate can be deduced ... Another gate (or an attached chamber?) may have occupied a position in the notched northeast segment of the east wall.

An elevated main hall, apparently the single structure within this compound, was raised near the north wall, some 70 m north of the putative south gate and equidistant from both edges of the platform. Its foundation block, 36 m wide and 25 m deep, was built prior to the surrounding platform. Columns on the foundation block were spaced at intervals of 3.8 m, nine running across the north and south faces, and four (double counting the end columns) at the east and west ends."[21]

This is a description of a fairly complex building, which probably was under some form of control by the elites or elders. Unfortunately, we don't know much about the exact use of the building. Experts presume it had a complex set of functions, from civic to religious. In any case, the

---

[21] Thorp, Robert L. "Erlitou and the search for the Xia."

large enclosed space inside the palace was enough for ten thousand people, so it's possible this space had religious and/or other social purposes.[22] Scholars infer this conclusion from early Chinese texts that come from the Zhou dynasty. For instance, in the *Book of Documents*, a collection of some of the oldest surviving texts from ancient China, it is mentioned that the "king ordered the multitude all to come to the courtyard." Thus, it is probable that was the purpose of Erlitou courtyards too.

Erlitou burial rites must have been fairly complex and once again testify to an intricate differentiation of social strata. In the richest tombs, various sorts of objects were found, such as bronze vessels, jade objects, ceramic jars and basins, pouring vessels, and the like. Weapons were also found, as well as a skeleton of a dog in a small coffin.

Inversely, numerous "slave" or "sacrifice" burials were found, presumably of people who were of lower status.

Needless to say, the Erlitou culture is best known for being one of the earliest to produce bronze objects. Numerous bronze cups were unearthed that were made of a thin layer of bronze molded from multiple pieces. The Erlitou people also learned to make bronze axes, knives, and bells, some of which were decorated with complex ornaments. Several bronze plaques with turquoise decorations were also found; they are further testaments to "quantum leaps" in metallurgical knowledge and skill.

Erlitou bronze tripod, the so-called *jue*. Some authors believe this was a wine vessel, and it's possible that it had a very specific ritual purpose. Part of the collection of the Archeological Research Institute of the Chinese Academy of Social Sciences.
Editor at Large, CC BY-SA 2.5 <https://creativecommons.org/licenses/by-sa/2.5>, via Wikimedia Commons; https://commons.wikimedia.org/wiki/File:CMOC_Treasures_of_Ancient_China_exhibit_-_bronze_jue.jpg

---

[22] Ibid.

But where does the legendary Xia fit? First, let's explore the historical documents mentioning the Xia. It's crucial to note that the legendary Xia didn't have a writing system, so any evidence of Xia has to be either archaeological or in subsequent writings. The Xia is mentioned in legends and myths that have found their way into later texts that came mainly from the Zhou period (some three thousand years ago).[23] The earliest historical evidence from ancient China (Shang dynasty) comes to us in the form of oracle bone inscriptions, which bear no mention of the Xia. Thousands of these oracle bones were found. They precede the Zhou dynasty by some five hundred years and are arguably closer to the mythical Xia, so it is curious that none of the unearthed bones mention the Xia. However, the bones do occasionally bear mentions of the Shang dynasty, so it is reasonable to assume that if the great Xia dynasty existed and been important, at least some bones would have contained inscriptions referring to the Xia, owing to its historical closeness to the Shang (and purported cultural continuity between the Xia and Shang). But so far, this hasn't been the case.

It is for this and other reasons that numerous scholars believe the Xia dynasty was a fabrication of the Zhou. But what would be the motive for this? Some scholars emphasize the parallels between the legendary Yu (who is reportedly the most important Xia ruler) and King Wen of Zhou, who were both instructed and guided by deities.[24] This kind of analogy might have served to "justify" the Zhou overthrow of the Shang, showing that it was mandated from the heavens. Needless to say, this is only a hypothesis. It's questionable whether the Zhou simply made up the whole story or whether they simply decided to focus on a specific legend that served their purpose. Some authors evoke the concept of "social memory" and that passages that mention the Xia have a purpose of preserving the memory of ancient times and societal changes, not necessarily the purpose of providing accurate historical accounts about a certain dynasty.[25] In this sense, the Xia can be a sort of "mnemonic" tool, a way to synthesize numerous historical events into one single culture and dynasty.

---

[23] Chen, Minzhen. "Faithful History or Unreliable History: Three Debates on the Historicity of the Xia Dynasty." *Journal of Chinese humanities* 5, no. 1 (2019): 78-104.

[24] Ibid.

[25] Ibid.

Now, we're at the same point as when we started our discussion o the Xia. The Xia dynasty exists somewhere in between myth and reality, legend and history. Some of the stories linked to the Xia are not without a historical basis, as we'll see in the next chapter on Yu the Great, the legendary Xia king. Hardships and achievements attributed to the Xia dynasty were most certainly things the ancient Chinese people experienced. On the other hand, it is still impossible to prove the existence of a culture or dynasty named Xia or the existence of a king named Yu the Great. Attempts have been made to establish a link between the Erlitou culture and the Xia, but the results are ambiguous at best. Any real existence of a king (or emperor) named Yu who propelled China into a period of exponential development is even more dubious. The developmental path ascribed to the Xia and Yu was most certainly trotted by the Chinese. But whether it was the Xia who were responsible for these developments is still questionable.

Chapter 3: Yu the Great

Now that we've cleared up (or further perpetuated) the question of the historicity of the Xia dynasty, let's look at Yu the Great, the legendary emperor of the Xia. As mentioned, the textual evidence for the Xia comes from a much later period, from the Zhou dynasty. These are exceedingly hermetic texts full of ancient cosmology and mythology. Before we move on to describe the achievements ascribed to Yu the Great, let's briefly explore his lineage.

The Xia supposedly come from ten totemic sun-birds who lived in the Mulberry Tree. All ten sun-birds rose from the Mulberry Tree and went westward to the western counterpart of their own Mulberry Tree. Then there was a man called Yellow Lord (Huang Di). Yellow Lord is a complex figure in his own right and is steeped in hermetic Chinese methodology, perhaps even more than his successor, Yu the Great. In some versions of the myth, he is credited as the ancestor of numerous tribes, including the Xia. His surname was either You Nai Shi or Han Yuan Shi, which is a testament to his totemic nature. In classical Chinese, *nai* can mean "three-legged turtle or dragon." *Han Yuan* is "black turtle," which has heavenly qualities. So, the Yellow Lord is an entity somewhere in between a totem and a human being.

The Yellow Lord had a wife named Lei Zu ("Woman of the Western Mound"), and the two had a son called Chang Yi, who inherited the kingdom of the Yellow Lord. Chang Yi is also associated with the west and with water. Chang Yi's home was the Ruo River, which flowed from the western version of the Mulberry Tree. According to one version of the myth, Chang Yi had a son named Han Liu. "Han Liu had a long throat and small ears, a human face with a pig's snout, a scaly body, thighs like wheel rims and pettitoed feet."[26]

Thus, Han Liu was a creature akin to a dragon, similar to Zhuan Xu (also spelled Zhuanxu), who was also Chang Yi's son, according to a slightly different version of the myth.

Moreover, both Han Liu and Zhuan Xu are associated with the Ruo River, which is their purported home. The descendants of Zhuan Xu are referred to as the people with three faces, who are immortal. He also had an adversary, Gong Gong. It seems that Gong Gong is accredited as the source of great floods, which the ancient Chinese (and people elsewhere) experienced, using it as the basis for their myths and legends. Zhuan Xu had a son, Gun, who attempted to solve the flooding problem but was unable to do so. The myth has it that Gun followed the signs of turtles and owls. Unfortunately for Gun, his solutions weren't effective, and he was executed by the king, who was probably his father. However, Gun's death wasn't his end, as he was transformed into *nai* (the aforementioned three-legged turtle or dragon). After that, his son, Yu (who would become Yu the Great), was born.

Similar to how Gun followed patterns laid out by turtles and owls, Yu followed the pattern of yellow dragons. He also built up a high land and led the digging of numerous canals to allow water to flow around settlements and not into them. This must have been an immense project that took years and an incredible human (and animal) workforce to complete. Yu the Great also led the dredging of riverbeds, which allowed for a more abundant water flow and perhaps even the increased navigability of rivers. Besides digging canals and dredging the riverbeds, Yu is credited with important reforms. For instance, he divided the country into nine provinces: Jizhou (冀州), Yanzhou (兗州), Qingzhou (青州), Xuzhou (徐州), Yangzhou (揚州), Jingzhou (荊州), Yuzhou (豫州), Liangzhou (梁州), and Yongzhou (雍州).

In a similar way to Gun, Yu also transformed into *nai*, a mythical being. After seeing him in his new form, Yu's wife, the Lady of Tu Mountain, ran away and turned into stone. It was only after this that she gave birth to Yu's son, Qi. The name "Qi" can mean "beginning," and

---

[26] Allan, Sarah. "The myth of the Xia Dynasty." *Journal of the Royal Asiatic Society* 116, no. 2 (1984): 242-256.

Qi is often credited as being the first hereditary ruler of China and the last to have a miraculous birth. Qi's son, Tai Kang, continued the Xia dynasty, which yielded many great kings. One of the last was a king named Kong Jia, about whom we have a little bit more information compared to other Yu's successors.

It seems that Kong Jia was the king who started the decline of the Xia. Kong Jia was interested in magic and the supernatural. The heavens sent him two dragons, but Kong Jia was unable to attend to them. One of them died. This dragon was unknowingly served as a meal to Kong Jia, who ate it, sealing his fate. In another version of the myth, the Xia ruler "dwelt at the Western River. Heaven had an ominous disaster: the ten suns came out together."[27] Soon, the Xia disappeared, only to be replaced by the Shang. It's not a coincidence that the ten suns were symbols of the Shang, and the ominous event that happened to the Xia ruler announced the arrival of a new dynasty, the first Chinese dynasty for which we have solid historical evidence.

---

[27] Ibid.

PART TWO: THE SHANG DYNASTY (c. 1600–1050 BCE)

Chapter 4: The Battle of Mingtiao

Although the decline of the Xia was visible from the time of Kong Jia, it was only with his successor, Jie, that the dynasty ceased to exist. A man called Tang finally overthrew the Xia in an act of open rebellion, which ended in the decisive Battle of Mingtiao. The battle was won by Tang, who became the first ruler of the Shang dynasty.[28] The battle is said to have taken place sometime around 1600 BCE. The Xia, as we've seen, became decadent, and even the heavens were sending signs of their upcoming demise. The end came in the form of Tang.

Perhaps there was more to Tang than simply being someone who represented the mandate of heaven. Some authors believe he was the leader of a widespread rebellion against the Xia and who might have, over time, become a sort of elite who governed the less-privileged people. In this sense, Tang could have been an expression of a wider rebellion against, for instance, the Xia dynasty's taxation and extravagance.

Unfortunately, we don't know the real circumstances of the Battle of Mingtiao. If there was something like a rebellion against the hegemony of the Xia, it's likely that numerous cultural groups participated and that Tang was simply one of the leaders.

---

[28] Mark, Joshua J. "Ancient China." *Ancient History Encyclopedia* (2012).

Tang

There's a very interesting tale about Tang preserved on bamboo slips that were discovered by the authorities as they were being smuggled into Hong Kong. These bamboo slips came from a much later period called the Warring States Period (5th to 3rd century BCE).[29] The story is called (somewhat poetically) "When Red Pigeons Gathered at Tang's House," and it goes like this. Tang was at his house when he saw red pigeons flocking on his roof. Tang took his bow and arrow and shot one pigeon, which he gave to his servant Xiaochen, ordering him to make a soup from the red pigeon. Xiaochen proceeded to make the soup, but before he was able to serve it to his master, Tang's wife, Ren Huang, arrived. Tang's wife wanted a taste of the red pigeon soup, but Xiaochen was hesitant. He was afraid that his master would find out and have him killed. But Ren Huang threatened to kill Xiaochen if he didn't let her taste the soup.

So, poor Xiaochen was forced to allow Ren Huang to taste the soup. After doing so, she was able to see all things in the world; her glance penetrated everywhere. Xiaochen took what was left of the soup, and he, too, experienced the same effects. Tang found out what happened, which prompted Xiaochen to flee to the Xia. Although he managed to run away from Tang, the Shang king enchanted Xiaochen, and the latter became very sleepy and was unable to pursue his plan. At that moment, a flock of ravens came to Xiaochen, wanting to eat him. However, they found out that Xiaochen couldn't be eaten. So, the leader of the ravens, a sort of spiritual medium, stepped in front and sent other ravens to the court of the Xia, where the Xia lord was making his offerings in the hope of gaining better health.

The spiritual medium raven possessed Xiaochen, which, in a way, negated the spell cast by Tang. The possessed Xiaochen reached the Xia, whose lord didn't know the reason for his own illness. But the possessed Xiaochen did know it: a man called Thearch employed black magic to make the Xia lord ill by ordering two white rabbits and two yellow snakes to dwell beneath the Xia lord's bedroom. Two mounds were also made beneath his bedroom. All these made the Xia lord ill.

---

[29] Allan, Sarah. "'When Red Pigeons Gathered on Tang's House': A Warring States Period Tale of Shamanic Possession and Building Construction set at the turn of the Xia and Shang Dynasties." *Journal of the Royal Asiatic Society* 25, no. 3 (2015): 419-438.

His heart wasn't working as it should have, and the lord's body started showing sores, which precluded him from resting.

The black magic items were removed, and the Xia lord regained his health. But one rabbit got away; to keep this rabbit away from the city, people started building parapets.

Needless to say, there are many ways to interpret this story. Sarah Allan, a scholar of ancient China, believes that this story takes the mythical content (Tang's magical powers, etc.) and blends it with the rites of building parapets to provide a sort of justification and historic-mythical basis for the rite.

Despite the Shang dynasty being the first Chinese dynasty for which we have actual written proof (found mainly on oracle bones), it is still steeped in myth. Studying Shang oracle bones and later textual evidence helped scholars to uncover an important founding figure, the minister Yi Yin. Similar to Xiaochen in the aforementioned story, Yi Yin was described as Tang's cook and someone who assisted in sacrifice rites. Some scholars believe that Yi Yin is a typical figure in ancient myths and legends of China. He was of low origins but was nevertheless brought up by the emperor and allowed to reach the highest office. It is also believed that such a motive stressed the importance of delegating or sharing power at the very top. The emperor was surely the top man, but he was unable to do anything unless he had support from the groups who were ruled by him.

In a very indirect way, the Yi Yin motif is a testament to the incredible cultural diversity of ancient China. As you might understand by now, there wasn't a simple succession of cultures; rather, China (and the world) had many cultures coexisting together. They probably engaged in extensive contact with one another, whether through trade or wars. It's likely that during certain periods, one or two cultures emerged as "leaders." To this day, China is an incredibly complex country with many different provinces, traditions, and ethnic groups. Back in the Bronze Age, it's likely that things were pretty much the same; perhaps, things were even more complicated and less centralized, considering the speed of communication and the transmission of knowledge. So, whoever was at the top had to be there with the approval of those he governed.

The Shang were at the top for quite a long time, owing to their cultural development, mastery of crafts, and willingness to learn from other cultures. We must not forget that the Shang cities were situated fairly close to the Erlitou sites, and there were likely extensive exchanges between the Shang and the Erlitou and between other ancient Chinese groups. The ingenious Shang, to whom we owe the very first written documents from ancient China, nevertheless encountered the same fate as the one they bestowed on the Xia. But let's first see their achievements before shifting to the decline of the Shang and the rise of the Zhou.

Chapter 5: Cultural and Military Developments

While most historians prefer to remain silent with respect to the Battle of Mingtiao, we know a lot more about one of the main protagonists of the battle: the Shang. The development of the Shang has been well preserved, and archaeologists have been able to track the early days of the Shang back to 2000 BCE.[30] The so-called "proto-Shang" were discovered in the Henan and Hubei provinces of China. In the early phases of development, the Shang inhabited modern-day Hubei; as time went on, they moved more to the south, crossing the Yellow River at one point and settling in modern-day Henan. It is presumed that the Shang went from a nomadic lifestyle, relying heavily on livestock, to a more agriculture-based, sedentary lifestyle.

---

[30] Hou, Liangliang, Yaowu Hu, Xinping Zhao, Suting Li, Dong Wei, Yanfeng Hou, Baohua Hu et al. "Human subsistence strategy at Liuzhuang site, Henan, China during the proto-Shang culture (~ 2000–1600 BC) by stable isotopic analysis." *Journal of Archaeological Science* 40, no. 5 (2013): 2344-2351.

Shang territory in the modern-day Chinese provinces of Hubei and Henan.
Lamassu Design Gurdjieff, CC BY-SA 3.0 <https://creativecommons.org/licenses/by-sa/3.0>, via Wikimedia Commons; https://commons.wikimedia.org/wiki/File:Shang_dynasty.svg

This leads us to the establishment of a very important Shang city called Zhengzhou. Zhengzhou is the name of a modern Chinese city situated at the old Shang archaeological site.[31] With the Zhengzhou site, we are probably entering the year 1600 BCE, so this ancient city might have been the first capital of the Shang dynasty after the legendary Xia were defeated. At Zhengzhou, a large wall made from rammed earth was discovered, measuring almost seven kilometers in length. But there are other Shang sites, such as Xiaoshuangqiao and Huanbei, which are both fairly large and surrounded by thick earth-rammed walls. The development of elaborate defensive structures shows that conflicts between groups were, more or less, a thing of everyday life in this period. Wealth and luxury had to be protected by any means possible. And while the Bronze Age, which was heralded by the Shang in ancient

---

[31] Guangkuo, Yuan. "The discovery and study of the Early Shang culture." *A companion to Chinese archaeology* (2013): 323-342.

China, brought very important developmental changes to humanity, it's quite likely there were some groups of people who simply wanted to "hijack" the developmental path and jump up a few steps by eradicating more advanced cultures and taking over their achievements.

The larger cities, almost by a rule, were surrounded by smaller settlements, which, in a way, orbited around the illustrious cultural centers. The surrounding settlements probably weren't exclusively "Shang." They probably had a very diverse mixture of people. In this light, the establishment of capital cities seems even more important, as it allows one to establish himself (and sometimes herself) as the "boss" in the area. The collection of tributes and taxes (if they existed back then) and more careful control of the area would also have been possible.

Social Hierarchy

To inspect the social hierarchy, we have to turn toward a place where, for all intents and purposes, the social hierarchy ceases to exist: death. But much like people aren't equal while they are alive, they don't cease being unequal in death. Ancient people were very careful to preserve the social hierarchy, even in the afterlife. The wealthiest members of the Shang were buried in large graves (around ten square meters). Wooden coffins were used to hold the bodies of the upper class, and some had both outer and inner wooden coffins. The coffins themselves were sometimes decorated or painted. Numerous prestigious objects were found in these graves. Archaeologists have discovered jade daggers, bronze tripods and jars, food containers, and bronze tools and weapons. Some graves of the elite also contained proto-porcelain.

As we move toward the bottom of the hierarchy, we uncover more modest graves that are smaller in size and usually contain ceramic objects. Some graves are smaller than one square meter, which means the body can only fit in a contracted, fetal-like position. These graves rarely have any objects.

The Shang were probably the first to start utilizing bronze on a larger scale. The aforementioned Erlitou culture was one of the first to produce bronze, but the use of bronze was restricted to a few types of fairly small objects, such as knives. The Shang, on the other hand, started using bronze for making tools like shovels and axes. Bronze shovels and axes are more effective than stone or wooden tools. Different bronze foundries were discovered in Shang settlements. There were probably many craftsmen specializing in smithing, and different workshops specialized in different types of tools. Moreover, there wasn't one single "recipe" for bronze. The proportion of copper and tin in the bronze alloy varies significantly. Some pieces of Shang bronze also contain lead, which is perhaps a testament to the willingness of the Shang to experiment and improve their metal further.

A bronze Shang ax that was possibly used for combat and ritual purposes.
Editor at Large, CC BY-SA 2.5 <https://creativecommons.org/licenses/by-sa/2.5>, via Wikimedia Commons; https://commons.wikimedia.org/wiki/File:CMOC_Treasures_of_Ancient_China_exhibit_-_bronze_battle_axe.jpg

In a similar way, there were numerous experts who made ceramics. They also aimed to improve their craft, which is why we are able to find the so-called "proto-porcelain" of the Shang.

This doesn't mean that some of the more ancient crafts were extinct by the time of the Shang. For instance, numerous bone workshops were uncovered. Animal and human bones were used for the production of all sorts of everyday objects, such as needles, arrowheads, rings, hooks, and the like. There has been some evidence of human sacrifice by the

Shang, so the use of human bones for the production of tools isn't that surprising. Interestingly, in such workshops, ivory was also found. It's likely the Shang had to import ivory from far away, meaning they had extensive communication with nearby cultures and much more distant ones.

Chapter 6: Politics and Religion

Probably the most important source of the Shang cultural practices are the famous oracle bones, which bear the first known writing system of ancient China. More than eight hundred oracle bones bear mentions of the Qiang, who were distinct from the Shang and probably subordinated to the latter.[32] The Qiang war captives had the grueling fate of being human sacrifices for the Shang. Although the exact reason behind the Shang dynasty's human sacrifices will probably remain obscure, there are ways to explain this phenomenon, all of which potentially bring insight into the religious and political system of the Shang.

A likely theory is that human sacrifices served as a way to legitimize the Shang dynasty's political control over the population. In this sense, the Shang (or any other ethnic group) cannot exist without positioning them in relation to other ethnic groups. The Qiang might have served as an antithesis of the Shang, providing a way for the Shang to establish themselves as the victors, the ones who exert power over others. This interpretation gives us a different kind of perspective on the topic of human sacrifice, which is important since modern people tend to ascribe such behavior to the depths of prehistory. People avoid interpreting this behavior, instead calling it pure barbarism, cannibalism, and the like.

The oracle bones probably had a complex purpose. They were likely used by the Shang in their court rituals in the following fashion.

---

[32] Shelach, Gideon. "The Qiang and the question of human sacrifice in the late Shang period." *Asian Perspectives* (1996): 1-26.

Alternative divinations were inscribed on a turtle shell, saying, for instance, "It will rain tomorrow" and "It won't rain tomorrow." Hot charcoal or another source of heat was then inserted into the previously hollowed-out parts on the back of the turtle shell. The hot charcoal inevitably made cracks in the turtle shell. The pattern of cracks with respect to the inscriptions was then interpreted by a diviner.[33] The exact content of the oracle bone inscriptions gives us a glimpse into the everyday worries and struggles of the Shang. "This night there will be no disaster." "The whole day we will not encounter great wind." "The whole day there will be no harm."[34] This content can be interpreted as not just predicting the future but also as a way to *affect* the future and, more importantly, free people from suffering.

In these rituals of the Shang, the early connection between religion and struggles with the environment is evident. And once again, we return to Freud, who believed that it was thanks to the harshness of the early environment of humans that deities came into existence. When a person has nothing to turn to, when they are completely at the mercy of environmental conditions, they might seek spiritual ways to improve their life.[35] The Shang oracle bones bear evidence of this initial struggle between humans and nature.

A pit containing numerous oracle bones excavated at Yinxu, Anyang, China.
Chez Câsver (Xuan Che), CC BY 2.0 <https://creativecommons.org/licenses/by/2.0>, via Wikimedia Commons; https://commons.wikimedia.org/wiki/File:Oracle_bones_pit.JPG

---

[33] Keightley, David N. "Shang divination and metaphysics." *Philosophy East and West* 38, no. 4 (1988): 367-397.

[34] Ibid.

[35] Freud, Sigmund. The future of an illusion. *Broadview Press*, 2012.

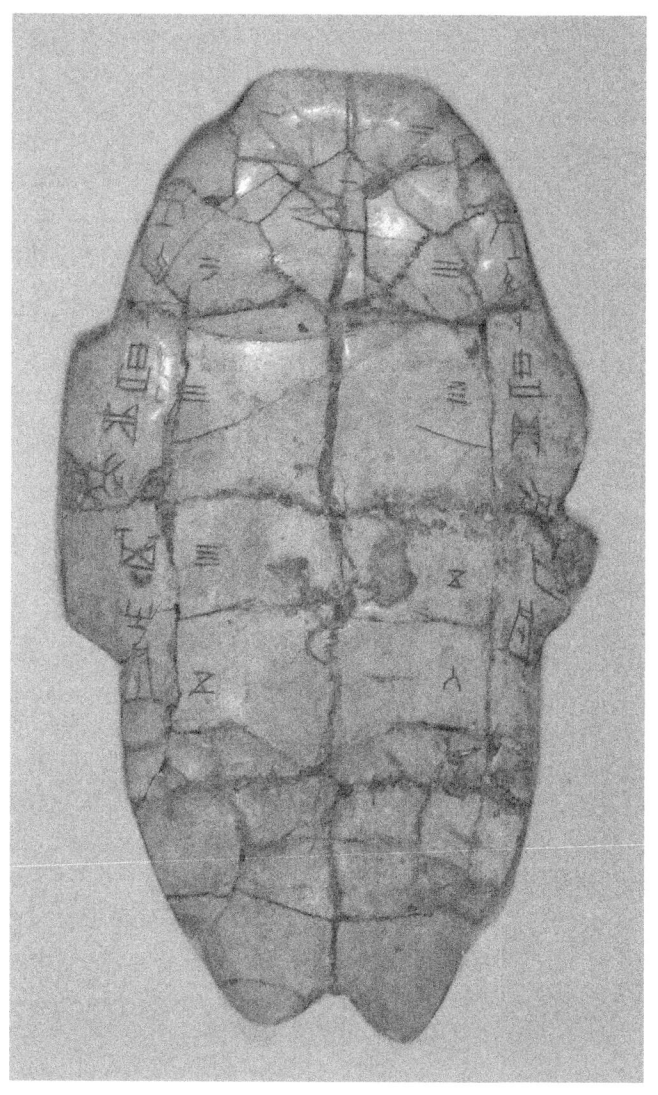

A very typical Shang oracle bone from a tortoise. This bone comes from the period of King Wu Ding. The two alternative predictions are interpreted as follows: "Gu divined: Ban will have misfortune" and "Gu divined: Ban will have no misfortune."
(National Museum of China, CC BY-SA 3.0 <https://creativecommons.org/licenses/by-sa/3.0>, via Wikimedia Commons; https://commons.wikimedia.org/wiki/File:Shang_dynasty_inscribed_tortoise_plastron.jpg

Let's now turn to a more concrete analysis of oracle bones related to the Qiang, which will help us uncover the mysteries of the Shang. You'll also understand just how much work goes into understanding even a single Chinese character preserved on oracle bones.

According to most scholars, the character pronounced as "Qiang" has the following meaning: "Western Rong sheep herdsmen."[36] The Qiang character is made from two separate characters, one denoting "man" and the other "sheep." The Qiang probably lived in northwest China and had a pastoral lifestyle. In that sense, they were on the periphery of Shang influence and were culturally distinct. Whereas the Shang were more agriculturally based, the Qiang were herdsmen. Thanks to their technological developments, notably the extensive use of bronze, the Shang were probably more effective soldiers and were able to keep the surrounding societies subjugated, at least for a certain amount of time. For instance, although chariots are absent from early Shang sites, they appear in the later period (around 1000 BCE) and must have been used in both war and hunting.

The Qiang weren't the only neighboring culture to be mentioned on oracle bones. In fact, dozens of societies are mentioned on oracle bones in a context that implies they enjoyed more or less extensive political freedom and autonomy from central Shang rule. Therefore, the structure of the Shang civilization wasn't entirely unlike the fiefdoms of the medieval age. Their domination over neighbors wasn't simply characterized by war and subjugation but also by negotiations and extensive cultural contact. For instance, the Shang nobles mixed with the nobilities of neighboring groups. Inversely, non-Shang were adopted into the clan or dynasty, and non-Shang were also able to take high political and religious positions.

There was certainly extensive trading going on between the Shang and their neighbors. The turtle shells for oracle bones were extensively procured from the outside. Other important materials, such as salt, tin, and copper, were also obtained from neighbors.

In this sense, the Qiang emerged as very important neighbors, at least for the Shang, since they are the only ones mentioned on oracle bones as being human sacrifices. The Qiang must have done something to precipitate a harsher response from the Shang.

At the site called Yinxu (Anyang), the biggest Shang city, numerous human sacrificial pits were excavated, with people sometimes accompanying the nobles in their afterlife. Although we don't know the ethnicity of the people found in these sacrificial pits, it's likely that the

---

[36] Shelach, Gideon. "The Qiang and the question of human sacrifice in the late Shang period. p. 4

Qiang war prisoners participated in similar rituals or were buried in the sacrificial pits found in Yinxu. What we do know for certain is that the oracle bones that mention the Qiang talk about the Shang and their allies hunting for the Qiang. The Qiang were often decapitated, at least according to the oracle bones, and numerous headless skeletons have been found in Shang sacrificial pits. Most of the people found in sacrificial pits were men, which further fosters the hypothesis that they were war captives.

But why did the Shang perform these rituals? Scholars are not certain, but there are some very likely hypotheses. For example, human sacrifices might have been a way to communicate with ancestors. This interpretation receives support from text discovered on oracle bones. Moreover, as is often the case with sacrifices, the Shang may have done them to please the spiritual beings who had power over human life. When the Shang noticed signs that harmony in the world was being lost, they might have felt compelled to offer something to the supreme spiritual beings to alter what seemed to be their impending annihilation.

But this is only a part of the story. To get the full picture, we have to turn toward the construction of the Shang state. At the top, of course, was a king surrounded by his noble family and members of the elite. The elites from other societies were allowed inside the Shang dynasty and vice versa. Below the elites was probably the military: somewhat wealthy people who had enough money to equip themselves for war and were directly controlled by the elites. Then came the craftsmen and artisans, who were of the utmost importance for cultural development. At the very bottom were (relatively) free farmers; they were probably the most numerous. It seems the Shang didn't have institutionalized slavery. In ancient Greece or Rome, war captives were often sold into slavery. The Shang didn't have institutionalized slavery, at least as far as we know, and thus had to find another "purpose" for their war captives.

Some Shang Kings

The Shang dynasty lasted for around six hundred years, and it is by no means possible to give a good account of all the Shang rulers here. However, we can turn to some of the more interesting stories about some of the Shang rulers, which were preserved in an ancient book called the *Records of the Grand Historian*, written by one of the first Chinese historians, Sima Qian (c. 145-86 BCE). In this book, Sima covers a period of around 2,500 years. Although Sima Qian is considered one of the first Chinese historians, the things he talks about have to be taken critically; this is very similar to other early historians, such as the Greek Herodotus, whose *Histories,* although incredibly interesting and captivating, isn't always completely reliable.

You may recall that the Shang story began with a ruler named Tang. At one point in Sima Qian's book, he writes the following words:

"After T'ang, when Emperor T'ai-wu came to the throne of the Shang dynasty, a mulberry and a paper mulberry sprang up together in the court of his palace and in the space of one night grew so large that a person could not reach around them with his arms. The emperor was frightened, but his minister I Chih said, 'Evil omens cannot prevail over virtue!' Then Emperor T'ai-wu strove for greater virtue in his rule and the two mulberries died. I Chih praised the emperor to the shaman Hsien. It was at this time that the shaman Hsien came to power."[37]

Many generations later came another Shang leader called Wu-ting. Sima Qian refers to him as someone who restored the Shang state and was dubbed the "Great Patriarch." He had a minister, Fu Yiieh, which is a regular theme in early Chinese history, with a king often having a very important minister who helps run the government. Sima sometimes refers to Wu-ting as someone who helped restore the Shang country, which might mean there was a period in which the Shang dynasty was threatened by external or internal enemies.

Unfortunately, the Shang experienced a similar decline as the Xia before them, and this time, the fate of Shang was sealed. According to legend, just five generations after the virtuous Wu-ting, King Wu-Yi went against the will of the spirits, and for this misdeed, the heavens sent thunder to kill him. The last Shang ruler, Di Xin, pejoratively referred to as Emperor Chou or Zhou, which can mean horse crupper (so, it is likely this nickname was a serious insult).[38] Sima Qian has a few words to say about Emperor Zhou, stating that people venerated this emperor while he was alive, but after he died, people had more respect for simple

---

[37] Qian, Sima. "Records of the Grand Historian of China" Available at: https://archive.org/stream/in.ernet.dli.2015.532974/2015.532974.records-of_djvu.txt

[38] A crupper is a sort of leash that goes around the horse's tail and prevents the saddle from sliding forward. Due to its position, this leash gets contaminated by excrement, hence its negative connotation.

farmers!

Unfortunately, we don't know exactly how and why Emperor Zhou was depraved. Sima Qian tells us that he was "licentious," but other than that, we don't know too much. Many stories have been ascribed to Emperor Zhou, which have him engaged in all sorts of immoral deeds. However, it's likely these are false stories aimed more to explain the downfall of Shang than to capture historical reality.

Chapter 7: The Fall of the Shang Dynasty

The Shang experienced the same fate as the one ascribed to the Xia: they were overthrown by a rising neighbor. And just as a grand battle signified the end of the Xia, another grand battle marked the end of the Shang: the Battle of Muye. We know comparatively quite a lot more about the Battle of Muye than about the Battle of Mingtiao. This is, of course, because the Battle of Muye is more recent, taking place by 1046 BCE. The Battle of Mingtiao happened around six hundred years earlier. By 1046 BCE, Chinese cultures had already adopted the use of writing.

The story of the Battle of Muye is as follows. While the Shang society was plunging deeper into decadence and decline, a new source of progress emerged, the Zhou. They lived west of the Shang in modern-day Shaanxi province.[39] In the next chapter, we'll talk more in depth about the Zhou culture and its development prior and after becoming the dominant culture in China. It's likely the Zhou were becoming more frustrated with their vassal-like position in relation to the Shang. The Zhou were skilled craftsmen and had effective weapons and fairly good military organization. It was only natural for them to start considering themselves worthy of leading the Chinese world. For now, suffice it to say that around 1046 BCE, the Zhou and Shang fought a decisive battle. Led

---

[39] LI, Xiaobing (ed.). "China at War: An Encyclopedia." ABC-CLIO, 2012.

by King Wu, the Zhou rushed toward the main Shang cities, numbering forty-five thousand infantrymen. The Zhou also had a well-developed cavalry, around three thousand cavalrymen. The Shang were much more numerous, numbering 170,000 men, most of whom were slaves.[40] The Zhou directly attacked the Shang infantry. After seeing their elites being decimated by the Zhou, the Shang slaves gave up, and a lot of them probably defected to the other side. The Shang emperor fled and soon committed suicide. The Shang state was abolished, as some scholars put it, and a new dynasty arose: the Western Zhou.

The Shang was the first Chinese culture to leave traces of a somewhat organized writing system. The oracle bone inscriptions are testaments to an extremely old writing system—only the writing systems of ancient Egypt and ancient Middle Eastern states (and perhaps the still undeciphered Linear A Minoan writing system) are older. The Shang era gave us an incredibly complex writing system, which served as a basis for the modern Chinese characters.

Hundreds of thousands (perhaps even millions) of years have passed since the emergence of a new, human-like species that dwelled on Earth in search of food and shelter. For thousands and thousands of years, people had relatively similar lifestyles, used relatively simple stone tools, and hunted and gathered the food they could find. Then, after a period of just a few thousand years, evidence of the New Stone Age is present, with more advanced stone-processing methods, domestication of animals, inceptions of a sedentary lifestyle, and agriculture. Add a few thousand years more, and we're in the Bronze Age. People learned how to combine different metals to craft more durable tools. They also became skilled agriculture workers, craftsmen, and soldiers. Then, as a crown to all these achievements, humans invented what's perhaps the greatest invention of all: writing systems.

The exponential nature of human development should be evident by now. But by talking about this, we also have to be aware of the proper historical context. Although the use of writing systems is an incredible

---

[40] Initially, the Shang didn't have institutionalized slavery. It seemed that as time went on, they relied more and more on slaves, and ultimately, they paid dearly for this. We can encounter similar examples of slavery-related problems throughout history. Sparta had a big problem in periods when the slaves drastically outnumbered the free population. Rome saw numerous slave revolts, some of which were extremely dangerous for the stability of the nation. In other words, slavery, besides being extremely unethical, turned out to be a not-so-wise business plan.

intellectual feat for beings that nine thousand years prior only knew how to craft simple stone tools, the ritual significance of early inscriptions is obvious. In China, the earliest inscriptions are inextricably linked to the spiritual universe. Writing something down was an act of creating a better future, an act of influencing unpredictable nature. In this sense, the early Chinese inscriptions are steeped in the mythical, religious, and spiritual. However, the writing didn't only have this purpose. Shang bronze vessels also have writing on them. Coming from the late Shang period, these bronze vessel inscriptions have a somewhat practical nature, although they are still steeped in the ritual world. They tell us about the name of the clan of the person who owned the (probably prestigious) bronze vessel and also the name of the craftsman who made it.[41]

Soon after the end of the Shang, the oracle bones almost completely disappear, and the writing is encountered in numerous other contexts. Perhaps this points to one of the reasons why the Shang disappeared in the first place. They weren't practical enough, and once they reached the top, they stagnated. The Zhou, who were maybe more practical at the time, took their chance and propelled China into a new era of development.

---

[41] Boltz, William G. "Early Chinese Writing." *World Archaeology* 17, no. 3 (1986): 420-436.

PART THREE: THE ZHOU DYNASTY (c. 1050–221 BCE)

Chapter 8: Western and Eastern Zhou Dynasties

The Zhou (or Chou) most certainly didn't come out of the blue. This culture existed and developed for a long time before it took over the helm of China. The early Zhou (c. 1400 BCE) lived in the Loess Plateau, which is an arid region just south of modern-day Mongolia. In the 2nd millennium BCE, the Loess Plateau was essentially a steppe, with forest vegetation here and there. The altitude of the original Zhou place of living was around one thousand meters above sea level. Over time, the Zhou started moving southward and eastward, reaching fertile regions surrounding the rivers.[42] It is possible the Zhou were compelled to move southeastward by two broad factors: migrations of nomads from the north and increasing climatic aridity. Due to these reasons, the Zhou decided to seek a better environment for themselves, finally settling in the Fufeng region (modern-day western Shaanxi), building the capital Qiyi there. They continued moving eastward, finally reaching and overturning the Shang dynasty around one thousand years before the birth of Christ.

---

[42] Huang, Chun Chang, Shichao Zhao, Jiangli Pang, Qunying Zhou, Shue Chen, Pinghua Li, Longjiang Mao, and Min Ding. "Climatic aridity and the relocations of the Zhou culture in the southern Loess Plateau of China." *Climatic Change* 61 (2003): 361-378.

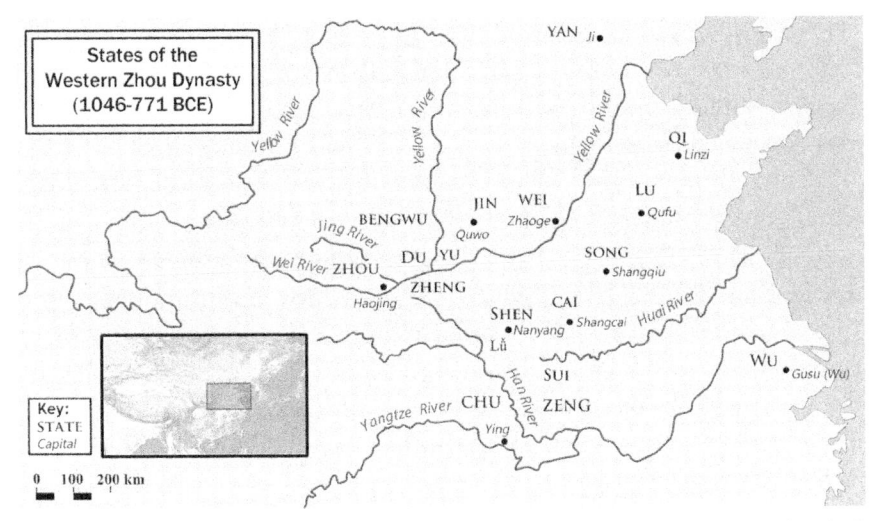

Map of Western Zhou and their neighbors. Note that this is only a rough estimate and took place over a fairly long period.

Philg88, CC BY-SA 3.0 <https://creativecommons.org/licenses/by-sa/3.0>, via Wikimedia Commons; https://commons.wikimedia.org/wiki/File:EN-WesternZhouStates.jpg

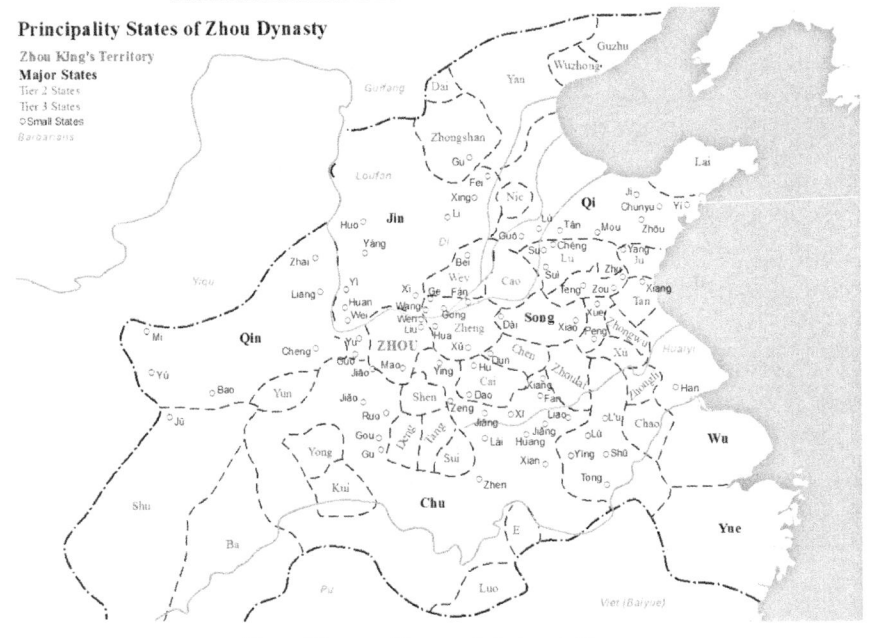

Map of Eastern Zhou and their neighbors.

SY, CC BY-SA 4.0 <https://creativecommons.org/licenses/by-sa/4.0>, via Wikimedia Commons; https://commons.wikimedia.org/wiki/File:States_of_Zhou_Dynasty.png

The Zhou adopted and modified the Shang writing system, and they brought their supreme deity, Tian, or Heaven, with them.[43] The mandate of heaven justified their overthrow of the Shang, much as the mandate of heaven oversaw the overthrow of the Xia by the Shang. From the early days of the Zhou, we find bronze vessels bearing inscriptions relating to this mandate of heaven or "Great Command from Heaven."

Initially, the Zhou settled in the more central regions of China, the aforementioned Shaanxi province. Their most important cities there were Zongzhou (Hao) and Fengjing (Feng or Fengxi), situated on the opposite banks of the Feng River, sometimes collectively referred to as Fenghao. It's likely that the Zhou emanated a sort of royal power from their prestigious cities, exerting authority over neighboring nations in a similar way as the Shang.

Unfortunately for the Western Zhou, which is how we refer to this initial period of the Zhou dynasty, their neighbors saw no reason not to do the same things as the Zhou. They invaded the wealthy cities and took on the role of leaders of the region. Finally, in 771 BCE, a group from the north, the Quan Rong, invaded the Western Zhou cities and killed King You (Gongsheng).[44] This occasion marks the end of the Western Zhou and the beginning of the Eastern Zhou.

As is always the case with the downfalls of great empires, there were many factors at play for the Western Zhou. It's possible that invaders from the west were catching up with them in terms of technology, weapons, and military organization. The Western Zhou likely grew comfortable with their position as a regional force and failed to make the necessary changes to stay on top.

The Eastern Zhou period is marked by the decreasing central authority of the royal family and the rise of powerful neighboring states. But even the Western Zhou established a sort of feudal system with their subordinate neighboring states, such as Ba, Zheng, and Yu.[45] During the Eastern Zhou, the importance and autonomy of neighboring states

---

[43] Rawson, Jessica. "Ordering the exotic: ritual practices in the late western and early eastern Zhou." *Artibus Asiae* 73, no. 1 (2013): 5-76.

[44] Khayutina, Maria. "Western Zhou cultural and historic setting." *The Oxford Handbook of Early China* (2020): 365.

[45] Childs-Johnson, Elizabeth, ed. *The Oxford Handbook of Early China*. Oxford University Press, USA, 2020.

further increased over the course of the so-called Spring and Autumn Period (771-481 BCE). With the Warring States Period (481-221 BCE), the aspirations of neighboring regions became even more prominent, and the period ended with the total defeat of the Zhou.

The Zhou Military

The Zhou owe their ascent to their powerful military. The elite members of the Zhou were inextricably tied to the military and must have served as the leaders of individual military units. They were likely also tasked with supplying their units with the necessary provisions. The Zhou probably had standing armies that were ready to act whenever necessary. The skill of archery was held in high esteem, and the elite members were supposed to be skilled archers. Furthermore, archery competitions were organized, and during the rule of King Mu, a sort of elite academy for archers was founded. The royal family regularly handed out beautiful bows and arrows to worthy individuals as a sign of allegiance and military prowess.

Thanks to advancements in the fabrication and processing of bronze, the Zhou were able to make durable chariots that were drawn by four horses (compared to the two-horse chariots of the Shang). Chariots had symbolic and practical purposes. They were used as a sign of wealth and status, not unlike people who use higher-end vehicles today to prove their elite status. However, chariots also had a very practical purpose. Chariot military units were formed, and they were able to wreak havoc among enemy infantry units. In fact, there's evidence that chariots were considered so dangerous that commanders would rather have them destroyed than have them fall into enemy hands. An interesting connection between ancient and modern wars can be made here.[46] Indeed, one of the implicit statements of this book is that modern societies aren't essentially different from societies established from the Neolithic Age onward.

During the period of the Eastern Zhou, the use of iron became more widespread use. For instance, graves from the Warring States Period hid numerous iron items, such as weapons and luxurious objects.[47] From

---

[46] In 1940, the British sank the French fleet docked at Mers-el-Kebir (then French Algeria) to prevent it from falling into German hands.

[47] Wagner, Donald B. "The earliest use of iron in China." *BAR International Series* 792 (1999): 1-9.

roughly the same period, iron foundries (for instance, in Hebei, central eastern China) were also unearthed, which are testaments to an organized, systematic production of iron in the 3rd century BCE. The Wu and Chu states possess the oldest traces of widespread iron use and production, with evidence of smelting processes being traced back as far back as the 5th century BCE. Interestingly, the oldest evidence of iron use comes from the Shang/early Western Zhou, and it has been proven that these iron artifacts have a meteoritic origin, meaning they literally came from space. The artifacts in question are bronze ax heads that were fostered with iron.

However, it is quite likely that the later production of iron in the Wu and Chu states and the propagation of iron across all of China are unrelated to the initial use of meteoritic iron. Around three centuries before the birth of Christ, iron reached the Zhou and quickly replaced bronze as the most-used metal for producing various items. There were possibly other sources of iron production, possibly from the northern steppe cultures. In fact, a grave was found in Shaanxi dating from the 6th century BCE containing gold-iron swords and knives. By this time, the Western Zhou were pushed eastward. The grave also contained evidence that corresponded more to steppe cultures. In other words, this must have been a cultural group under the influence of both the steppe and Chinese cultures.

In the early days of experimentation with iron (8th century BCE), iron wasn't of good quality and must have been inferior to bronze. It was possibly used as decoration for prestigious weapons. It was only in the 6th century BCE that more durable iron was produced in the southern states of Wu and Chu. The smithing techniques of Wu and Chu were related to the production of bronze agricultural tools. It's possible that during these early days, iron products were fairly brittle, though fairly resistant to wear and tear, compared to bronze. But China wouldn't have to wait long for the perfection of iron production.

The Zhou made other important breakthroughs, such as the use of the crossbow. The crossbow was used by Chinese militaries during the Warring States Period, which lasted from the 5th to the late 3rd century BCE.[48] Presumably, a man, Chi'in Shih, from a state called Chu invented the crossbow, probably during the 6th century BCE. The crossbow

---

[48] Cartwright, Mark. Crossbows in Ancient Chinese Warfare. *World History Encyclopedia*.

entered, relatively speaking, widespread use, as it was adopted by other states. For instance, the military of the state of Qi also adopted the crossbow by the time of the Battle of Maling (341 BCE), and it was thanks to crossbows that they won the battle against the Wei state.

Needless to say, it wasn't easy to make a good crossbow back then, and it must have been fairly expensive. This is why only chosen and well-trained soldiers were bestowed with the opportunity of using crossbows. For the most part, the Chinese militaries were fairly standard with the infantry typical of the period.[49]

---

[49] Greeks and Romans used crossbow-like weapons during roughly the same period. Greeks had their *gastraphetes*, and Romans had their large *ballista*. It's not clear whether there is a connection between Chinese and European crossbow-like weapons, as is often the case with ancient connections between Europe and the Far East.

Chapter 9: Cultural Developments

The most important historical evidence from the Zhou period comes in the form of bronze vessels bearing different sorts of inscriptions. In this sense, the discovery of more than one hundred bronze vessels in a single pit by farmers in 1977 near Mount Qi in the Fufeng region was instrumental since it provided archaeologists and linguists with an abundance of material to work with.[50]

More specifically, 103 bronze vessels were found there, and 74 had inscriptions. It seems they all came from a single line of craftsmen-scribes, the Wei family. The Wei family is presumed to have originated within the Shang elite, but they became integrated into the Zhou after the latter defeated the Shang. One particular bronze vessel, a water pan cast by a man named Qiang, is particularly interesting since it bears what some scholars refer to as the first conscious attempt in China to write history. The pan is famous among archaeologists and is usually referred to as the "Shi Qiang pan." It was presumably made around 900 BCE.

---

[50] Shaughnessy, Edward L. *Sources of Western Zhou history: inscribed bronze vessels*. Univ of California Press, 1992.

The famous Shi Qiang pan. Below is the translation of the inscriptions on the vessel. Also, note the drastic progress in the quality of bronze objects from the Erlitou to the Zhou. Located in the Baoji Bronzeware Museum.

幽灵巴尼, *CC BY-SA 3.0 <https://creativecommons.org/licenses/by-sa/3.0>*, *via Wikimedia Commons*; *https://commons.wikimedia.org/wiki/File:Shi_Qiang_pan.jpg*

Here is a portion of what was inscribed on the pan:

"Accordant with antiquity was King Wen! (He) first brought harmony to government. The Lord on High sent down fine virtue and great security. Extending to the high and low, he joined the ten thousand states.

Capturing and controlling was King Wu! (He) proceeded and campaigned through the four quarters, piercing Yin and governing its people. Eternally unfearful of the Di (Distant Ones), oh, he attacked the Yi minions.

Model and sagely was King Cheng! To the left and right (he) cast and gathered his net and line, therewith opening and integrating the Zhou State.

Deep and wise was King Kang! (He) divided command and pacified the borders.

Vast and substantial was King Zhao! (He) broadly tamed Chu and Jing; it was to connect the southern route.

Reverent and illustrious was King Mu! (He) patterned (himself) on and followed the great counsels."[51]

---

[51] Shaughnessy, Edward L. Sources of Western Zhou history: inscribed bronze vessels. Univ of California Press, 1992. p. 4

The scribe Qiang goes on with his odes to the Zhou royal family and ends with a brief mention of himself. He writes about his hopes for a long life adorned with wealth, which would allow him to serve the Zhou in the best way possible.

In general, the bronze vessel inscriptions regularly mention the Zhou royal family and the fact that it was chosen to rule. The Zhou rulers were presented as "stabilizers" or "protectors" of their region. Much like the Shang, they were connected to the neighboring elites through political marriage. It seems the kings were considered the absolute owners of all the lands; although this might have been the case, once the lands were granted to the elites, they probably had almost absolute power over the land and even the right to exchange or sell it.

Agriculture permeated practically all aspects of life during the Zhou period. Not only was it a major source of food and wealth, but it was also the essence of numerous Zhou rituals. In turn, the proper observance of rituals was related to the well-being of the royal family and the whole state. A major ritual involved ceremonial plowing, in which the elites had to participate personally. A large piece of land called "Thousand Acres," as ancient texts have it, was dedicated specifically for these ritual purposes. Moreover, the bronze vessels were a major part of the rituals and a crucial connection between the royal family and the elites. Namely, the heads of neighboring states were required to prove their subordination in periodic rituals in the Zhou court, and in return, the Zhou kings gifted their "vassals" with beautiful bronze vessels.

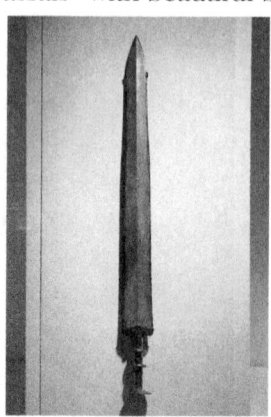

A bronze sword from the Eastern Zhou dynasty. The blade is still fairly sharp, testifying to the perfection of bronze production in the later period of the Zhou.
Editor at Large, CC BY-SA 2.5 <https://creativecommons.org/licenses/by-sa/2.5>, via Wikimedia Commons; https://commons.wikimedia.org/wiki/File:CMOC_Treasures_of_Ancient_China_exhibit_-_bronze_sword.jpg

For all intents and purposes, the Zhou emanated an allure of prestige, luxury, and dominance. They were able to accumulate large amounts of wealth and used this wealth to ensure their own status. Powerful women who owed their influence to their wealth and social status and not necessarily to military prowess started to emerge. For instance, Queen Wang Jiang seems to have been very influential in the court, as she directed various political activities and relationships of the royal house. In other words, the women during the Zhou period weren't simply an exchange currency or a guarantee of connections between the Zhou and their neighbors.

Philosophical Developments

Over the course of the Zhou era, especially during the Spring and Autumn Period and the Warring States Period, numerous philosophical schools of thought were developed. Scholars sometimes refer to the period between 550 and 200 BCE as the "Hundred Schools of Thought" or "Hundred Philosophers."[52]

Confucius is by far the best-known philosopher from this period, and he proved to be one of the most important influences on Chinese philosophy in general, akin to the way Plato and Aristotle shaped European philosophy. Confucius was a strong believer in benevolent leadership, cherishing the "sage-king" ideal personified in legendary emperors of prehistoric China.[53] One of Confucius's ideas was personal virtue. An absolute ruler's virtue should transpire through the whole community, meaning that if the ruler was virtuous, the people he led would be willing to abide by the rules and be good subjects.

Confucius wasn't born in the state of Zhou. He came from the state of Lu (modern-day Shandong province), one of the states (nominally) subordinate to Zhou. He was born around 551 BCE. Confucius was a master of a number of skills and arts that were considered essential during the period, such as music, archery, calligraphy, arithmetic, and charioteering. He must have known numerous works of art and science by heart, which was, generally speaking, a must for ancient scholars.

---

[52] Tu, Wei-Ming. "Confucius and Confucianism." Confucianism and the Family: A Study of Indo-Tibetan Scholasticism (1998): 3-36.

[53] It's an incredible coincidence that Plato was writing his famous *Republic*, where he too formulated his ideas about benevolent leaders and sage-kings, roughly during the same period as Confucius.

Confucius was also one of the early teachers in China. There were surely many teachers before him, but Confucius was probably one of the first to consciously choose this way of life, with the goal of improving individuals and society as a whole. One of the ways to do this was to teach sons of noble people and improve them as people, thus providing the basis for just and virtuous leadership.

Confucius's method was in stark contrast with the hermits, who were also known as wise men but chose to abandon society. Confucius wanted to improve his society for the better and was intensely involved in political debates of the day. He was involved in the government's public works and served as a minister of justice. After serving the state of Lu for some time, he left his home state, somewhat disillusioned by the royal lifestyle of the Lu elite. He toured China, and it is thanks to this that he became well known, even during his days. By the time of his death (c. 479 BCE), he amassed around three thousand people who defined themselves as his followers.

One of the most important Confucian scriptures, the *Analects*, captures the discourse and reasoning of Confucius as it must have been received by his followers. In the *Analects*, we encounter Confucius, who is very close to a saint (he was often revered as such by the Chinese population in the centuries to come). In this sense, Confucius is similar to Socrates. Both were seen as being more than sages and men with incredible mastery over themselves. Like Socrates, Confucius didn't exert his intellectual influence upon his followers; his spiritual influence was just as important.

Confucius had a vigorous and inquisitive mind, and he was always thinking about ways to improve himself and learn new things. In the *Analects*, he says, "It is these things that cause me concern: failure to cultivate virtue, failure to go deeply into what I have earned, inability to move up to what I have heard to be right, and inability to reform myself when I have defects."[54]

During roughly the same period, a counterpart to Confucianism emerged called Taoism. While Confucianism dealt with concrete issues of living in a state, improving oneself, and becoming virtuous, Taoism was more concerned with the philosophy of nature. Taoism is an incredibly complex cluster of religious and philosophical viewpoints, and

---

[54] Tu, Wei-Ming. "Confucius and Confucianism." p.11

it was developed for centuries. Instead of diving deep into the diversity of Taoism teachings and its perplexing history, we will only note that it is, in a way, more esoteric than Confucianism since it deals with the underlying principles of the whole universe.

Legalists were another group of ancient Chinese intellectuals who stood in stark contrast to both Confucians and Taoists. Legalists were influenced by the political instability of the Warring States Period and formulated justifications for autocratic systems. For instance, Legalists were behind the autocratic regime of the Ch'in state, which, in turn, served as the basis for the establishment of the empire and fostering the position of the emperor. Legalists gave practical advice concerning the surveillance of the population and punishment of anti-government actions.

Consider the following excerpt from the work of Li Si, who relied heavily on the founders of the Legalist school of thought, Shen-tzu and Han-tzu:

"Wise rulers alone are capable of dealing severely with those who commit minor crimes, [making it clear that] even minor crimes are severely punished and that much more severely would those who commit major crimes be dealt with. Consequently, the people dare not transgress ... As a wise sovereign rules autocratically, authority does not reside in the hands of his ministers. Only then can he obliterate the path of virtue, muzzle the mouths of fast eloquence, curb the deeds of high-spirited men, keep the empire in ignorance, and exercise his faculties of seeing and hearing by himself alone."[55]

In other words, the Legalists were concerned with fostering the central government and the position of the supreme ruler. In their opinion, power should be much more personal and concentrated in the hands of a single man. It is easy to feel dismayed at such words, but we have to put them in their historical context. During the Warring States Period, numerous Chinese states battled for supremacy. This period determined who would lead China in the centuries to come. Under such circumstances, the Legalists provided the philosophical basis for the flourishing of imperial, absolutist tendencies, as they believed a single centralized ruler would be the only one capable of putting an end to the

---

[55] Hsiao, Kung-chuan. "Legalism and autocracy in traditional China." *Chinese Studies in History* 10, no. 1-2 (1976): 125-143.

civil wars.

There was another important intellectual contribution to Chinese culture during this time: Sun Tzu's *The Art of War*, probably one of the most famous books ever written. Sun Tzu lived in the 6th century BCE, just before the Warring States Period. *The Art of War* shows just how much warcraft had progressed, even before the Warring States Period, by which time China must have already witnessed numerous armed conflicts. It took some time, from the early Neolithic Age to the ripe Iron Age, for people to perfect the craft of organized warfare. The primary incentives for war—gaining new lands and wealth, development of solid weapons, and strife for prestige—all converged by the latter half of the 1st millennium BCE in China, and the scene was set for a great war, one that would determine China's future. But before we move on to describe this period (the end of the Zhou and the emergence of the Qin), we'll briefly focus on *The Art of War*, which will give us a nice basis for thinking about the Warring States Period.

The very first words of Sun Tzu in *The Art of War* are, "The art of war is of vital importance to the State."[56] However, this book isn't an ode to war. It's a very rational and practical guide on how to wage war and, most importantly, how to avoid battle when possible. For instance, Sun Tzu tells us that, when possible, it's better to avoid besieging walled cities. The setting up of a siege takes a lot of time, and then an army will need even more time to try and break into the city, by, for instance, making a mound against the city walls. Moreover, he tells us that it's always better to take a country while keeping it intact, and it's better to capture a group of soldiers than to battle them.

Then we have advice on how many miles an army can cover on a daily basis and when and how men should march without most of their equipment so they can move faster. Sun Tzu also valued proper reconnaissance; he believed that no army should be moved anywhere before the terrain was properly investigated. In addition, Sun Tzu talks positively about the use of different types of signals, such as flags, banners, signal fires, and drums, to remain in control of the army.

Sun Tzu's *The Art of War*, in a way, is a collection of loosely related sayings, each of which is a few lines long. In other words, this is not

---

[56] Tzu, Sun. The Art of War. Available at:
https://sites.ualberta.ca/~enoch/Readings/The_Art_Of_War.pdf

necessarily a completely coherent system for leading an army but more like a collection of wise statements that any general should have in his memory. One of our favorite lines from this book is, "When you surround an army, leave an outlet free. Do not press a desperate foe too hard." This is an incredibly concise yet rich statement, pertinent not only to warfare but also to human relationships in general. This is the reason Sun Tzu's work is admired even today, some 2,500 years of military development later. He was not only a supporter of good reconnaissance but also supported the use of spies. It is at this point that Sun Tzu's sane, practical spirit comes to the forefront: "Knowledge of the enemy's dispositions can only be obtained from other men." According to Sun Tzu, the spiritual world has no place in warfare. Too often, omens and prophecies turn out not to be true.

Chapter 10: Fall of the Zhou Dynasty

By the 5th century BCE, the authority of the Zhou was crumbling. Inversely, the influence of the Han, Wei, and Zhao states increased, and the Zhou were forced to officially recognize these three states so they could take a more active part in defending the Zhou in their constant struggles against northern and western invaders, such as the Xiongu and Loufan who were threatening the Zhou and other Chinese states from the north or the Qiang who were coming from the west. When the armies of these (and other) states grew strong enough, and at the moment the Zhou were no longer able to force the neighboring states back into submission, the Warring States Period started. It was a sort of free-for-all battle that lasted for centuries.[57] As the 4th century BCE was setting its foot on the scene of history, four more states emerged: Qi, Qin, Chu, and Yao. There were many other smaller states, but the three mentioned before (Han, Wei, and Zhao), together with Qi, Qin, Chu, and Yao, were the most powerful and tended to absorb the smaller ones. Alliances, truces, skirmishes, and open wars were extremely numerous, hence the name of the period.

The scale of warfare in this period is staggering and probably unmatched by almost anything that was happening in Europe during

---

[57] Cartwright, Mark. Warring States Period. *World History.* Available at: https://www.worldhistory.org/Warring_States_Period/

roughly the same period.[58] The sheer size of armies and battles in this period shows us two things: the incredible fertility of the Chinese land and the high civilizational development of China, which was able to feed, arm, and, in some instances, pay many soldiers. It's possible that in some states, for instance, Qi and Qin, the number of infantry soldiers was close to one million.

The Qin were allies of the Zhou, who somehow clung to their old glory for most of the Warring States Period. In the 4th century BCE, the Qin still defended (to a certain extent) the interests of the dying Zhou state. But soon, they, too, would turn against their old masters. Numerous other states had ambitions similar to the Qin. The great Zhou were growing weaker, and power was simply waiting for someone worthy enough to come and grab it.

The Zhou were extremely important for the development of Chinese culture. Zhou cities served as centers of cultural development. The Zhou made important breakthroughs, and their great cities served as a place where different cultural influences met and gradually formed the cradle of Chinese culture. This finally materialized in the form of a precarious balance between the authority of the Eastern Zhou and developing neighboring states, which, after a while, made their own grand entrance into history. The Zhou inherited the bronze culture from the Shang and granted their successors a well-developed iron culture.

---

[58] Herodotus, for instance, gives very high numbers for the Greco-Persian Wars (5th century BCE), while modern historians tend to think critically about the hundreds of thousands of Persians who allegedly invaded Greece. In later years, the number of fighters in the Punic Wars, which saw tens of thousands of soldiers on each side, was perhaps more likely, although Polybius, our main source for the Punic Wars, sometimes exaggerates.

PART FOUR: THE QIN DYNASTY (221–206 BCE)

Chapter 11: Rise of the Qin Dynasty and Qin Shi Huangdi

Although the Qin lasted for a significantly shorter amount of time in comparison to previous dynasties, they were nevertheless very important for the development of the concept of an "empire" and an "emperor." The Qin started the long tradition of Chinese emperors.

But let's start with the basics. The Qin were situated, roughly speaking, in the area previously controlled by the Zhou (modern-day Shaanxi province). It is extremely challenging to speculate about the ethnicity of the Qin, though it's likely that they were initially perceived as barbarians but slowly adopted the cultural achievements of the Zhou (and other states) and also worked on their own cultural achievements.

As mentioned, they were initially allies of the Zhou, with Duke Xin, the Qin ruler in the 4th century BCE, being awarded his title by the Zhou for protecting their interests. The Qin rulers were also influenced heavily by the Legalist tradition, which provided a sort of ideological backing for later territorial expansions. But by the 3rd century BCE, the Qin had initiated conflicts with the Zhou, and the Qin took over the remainder of the Zhou by 260 BCE.

Zheng rose to the Qin throne in 246 BCE when he was only thirteen years old. He was the son of the Qin king and a concubine that the king had met while in captivity in the state of Zhao. It may seem that Zheng might have been an unlikely successor due to being a son of a concubine, but direct royal lineage wasn't the only important thing in Chinese dynasties, and concubines had an important influence on the lives of many emperors.

Eight years after Zheng ascended the throne, in 234 BCE, Li Si was appointed as the Qin prime minister. The Qin now had two very capable and ambitious gentlemen at the wheel. Spurred by the recent subjugation of the Zhou, the Qin went on to subjugate other important states, such as Han (230 BCE), Wei (225 BCE), Yan (222 BCE), and Qi (221 BCE). Centuries of civil conflicts, coupled with a political and ideological vacuum that was coming to the forefront as the Zhou were growing weaker, made room for a different political system and a different ideology. Legalism, the ideological foundation of the Qin, which favored dictatorial, centralized control of subordinated states and the formation of a cult of personality, was a very logical product of the Warring States Period. After centuries of conflicts, countless broken alliances, and unstable truces, Legalism came as a breath of fresh air and a herald of newfound stability.

Qin was not the only state that looked favorably on Legalist scholars; other states also grasped the importance of this new stream of thought. But the Qin had both symbolical and real power manifested in their subjugation of the Zhou and their military power, which, coupled with strict Legalist ideology, were enough for the formation of the first Chinese empire.

Moreover, it's not a coincidence that young Zheng of Qin would become the first Chinese emperor. Often, we see an unfathomable and insatiable thirst for control in people who ascend to power when young. It's as if those who are revered and feared by their subordinates have no other path in life than to pursue their grandiosity. Sometimes, this results in debauchery, vice, and utter decadence. But Zheng was of a different breed. He was a capable leader with grand aspirations, becoming the first Chinese emperor. Sima Qian, who was far from favorable with Zheng, sometimes referred to him as "possessing the mind of a tiger or wolf."[59] Sima Qian nicely summarized the age of the Qin as the "World of Bronze," alluding to the prevailing power of arms over culture. Sima Qian juxtaposed the "World of Bronze" with the "World of Bamboo," a

---

[59] Feng Kai & Liu Lu, The stigmatized Qin Shihuang and the formation of Han culture, Qin Han studies, 2019 (00), pp.297-306.

world of culture, knowledge, and morals. While bronze was used for crafting arms, bamboo was an important source of writing material, hence its association with culture.[60]

As we've seen, by the year 221 BCE, all the other warring states had come under the control of the Qin. The leader of the Qin, Zheng, became the first Chinese emperor, gaining the title of Shi Huangdi, which literally means the "first emperor." The way he dealt with neighboring states was starkly different compared to how the Zhou dealt with their vassals. Shi Huangdi ordered the complete disarmament of subjugated states. Arms were collected, most certainly not without occasional quarrels and unrest, and brought to the Qin capital (Xianyang). The arms were then melted and used for making things, such as bells and statues.

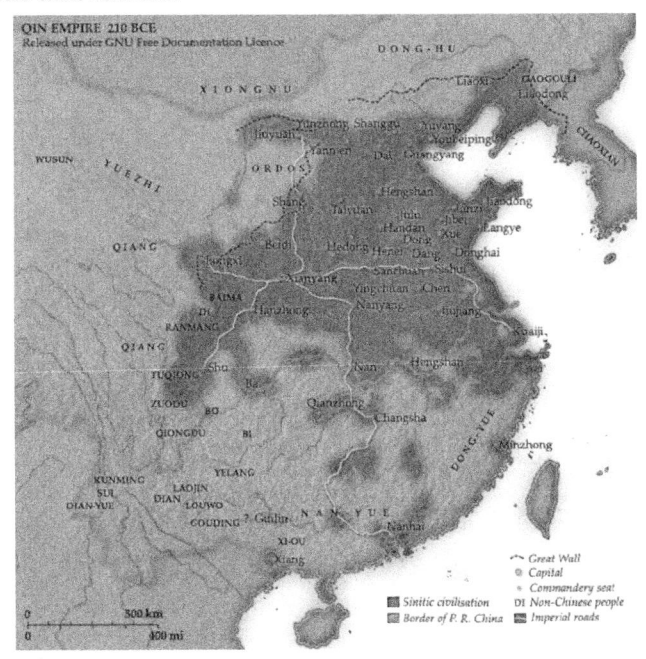

Map of the Qin dynasty at its height.
I, PHGCOM, CC BY-SA 3.0 <http://creativecommons.org/licenses/by-sa/3.0/>, via Wikimedia Commons; https://commons.wikimedia.org/wiki/File:QinEmpireWithOrdos.jpg

---

[60] Berkowitz, Alan. "Worlds of Bronze and Bamboo: Sima Qian's Conquest of History." (2001): 600-606.

Chapter 12: The Expansion of China and the Fall of the Qin Dynasty

Emperor Zheng didn't stop with the "unification" of China or, better put, the formation of the first Chinese empire. He conquered new lands that had been regarded as "barbaric" by the Zhou cultural sphere. Soon after becoming the emperor, he launched an invasion of modern-day southern China. The scene for virtually all events recounted up until this moment was modern-day north-central China. But with Emperor Zheng, the empire expanded its borders toward the south.

There were also northern conquests that were aimed primarily at putting an end to the perennial Chinese problem of northern invasions. These conquests were a prerequisite for the Great Wall of China and were led by a very important individual, General Meng Tian, who was directly appointed as the chief commander by the emperor. It is true that during the Warring States Period, various states started building large defensive walls to stop enemy forces from entering the country. Meng Tian probably took what was already available and built new fortifications, stabilizing the empire, at least against an external enemy.

However, internally, there were many struggles. As is often the case when a strong, charismatic, and authoritative leader dies, it's hard to fill his place, especially when the court is full of treacherous individuals. Qin Shi Huangdi died in 210 BCE due to an illness; he was around fifty years old at the time. Although he managed to avoid multiple assassination attempts, he couldn't run away from fate. Some scholars even believe that he desired to find the elixir of eternal life, which was what killed him since mercury was thought to be an important ingredient. It's possible that Qin Shi was poisoned by mercury, which prematurely ended his life.

When Emperor Zheng died in 210 BCE, he wasn't succeeded by Fusu, his oldest son, but by his second eldest son, Ying Huhai, later known as Qin Er Shi ("Qin the Second"). It's likely that a very powerful man and Emperor Zheng's previous advisor and chancellor had a hand in this. His name was Li Si. He was possibly one of the most important people in the empire's establishment and the administrative and government changes that were necessary for that establishment.[61] It's likely he played a role in the dubious events that came just after the death of the first emperor, namely the deaths of the emperor's oldest son, Fusu, and the military commander Meng Tian. Li Si was also involved in the appointment of Ying Huhai as emperor. The younger successor must have been easier to control compared to the older brother. Huhai must have had his own interest in becoming the emperor independent of Li Si, so we should not reject Huhai as an important factor in the removal of Fusu and Meng Tian, although these events will unfortunately remain clouded by the mists of time.

Unfortunately for Li Si, other people eyed his place as the empire's chancellor, and he was executed when various charges against him, including the capital charge of treason, were raised by the new chancellor, Zhao Gao, in 208 BCE. Zhao Gao, in turn, was able to remove Qin Er Shi. The emperor suffered the same fate as his older brother and Meng Tian, both of whom were forced to commit suicide. Qin Er Shi committed suicide in 207 BCE.

Ziying (or Liying) came to the throne not as an emperor but as a king under the watchful eye of Zhao Gao. This shows us just how much the influence of the Qin was reduced after the death of the first emperor. His exact relationship with previous emperors isn't clear, and he might have been either Fusu's son, the second emperor's brother, or the first emperor's nephew.[62] Ziying had Zhao Gao assassinated a few days after

---

[61] Kulmar, Tarmo. "On the nature of the governing system of the Qin Empire in ancient China." *Folklore: Electronic Journal of Folklore* 59 (2014): 165-178.

[62] Goldin, Paul Rakita, ed. *Routledge Handbook of Early Chinese History*. Routledge, Taylor & Francis Group, 2018. p. 146-159.

he was appointed as the king. But Ziying didn't rule for a long time (according to some sources, he ruled for only forty-six days).

The neighbors of the Qin, which were recently subjugated by the Qin, took their chance and attacked the weakened empire. The Han leader, Liu Bang, penetrated into Qin territory and defeated the imperial army. Ziying's life was spared, but he was not alive for long, as another important warlord, Xiang Yu of the Chu, had Ziying and his whole family executed in 206 BCE.

Chapter 13: Cultural Developments

Under the leadership of Li Si, basic economic matters were brought into order. For instance, Li Si heralded the standardization of the coinage system, as well as the closely related weight and measuring systems. The Chinese states had their own coins of various kinds before, but it was from 221 BCE and with Li Si that an organized, systematic production of standardized coins, weights, and measures was initiated. Moreover, Li Si (or his government) understood the importance of standardizing the writing system, which allowed for more seamless written communication within the vast empire.

These factors served as the basis for a relatively short period of economic well-being during the first Chinese empire. After centuries of conflicts, people could finally enjoy peace and accumulate wealth. The empire itself, needless to say, benefited from this and launched important projects, such as the aforementioned Great Wall. The Qin didn't build the Great Wall as it stands today. But the concept of the Great Wall and the initial (though very grandiose) constructions, which, at the time, must have been enough to keep invaders away, were started by the Qin and, more specifically, by the first emperor.

During the Warring States Period, the Qin mastered the employment of large masses of people for military purposes. Now they employed large masses of people to build the Great Wall. The building of the Great Wall wasn't really that much safer than war, and it's likely that thousands of people died as a result of being forced to work on it.

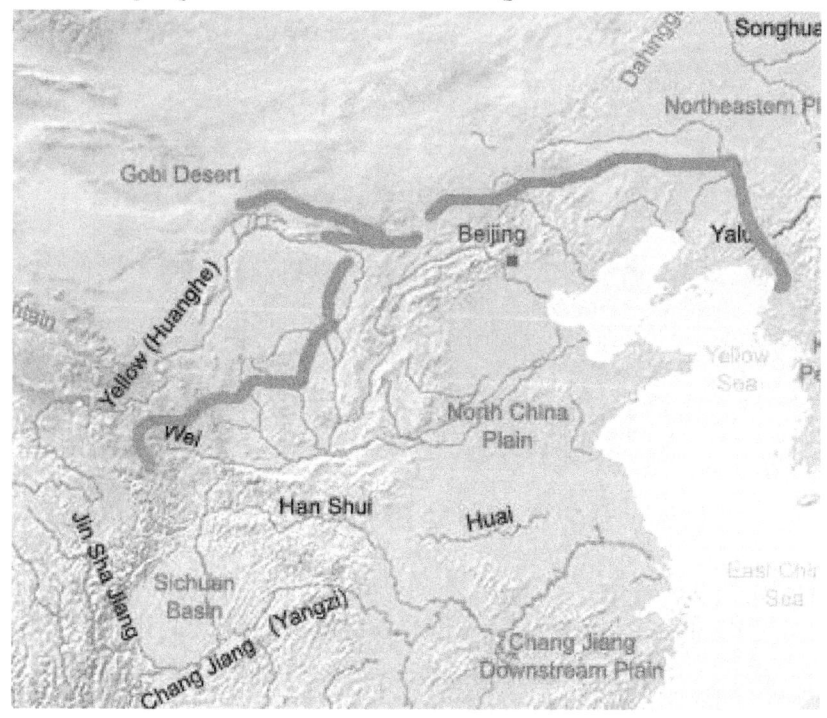

Walls built during the Qin dynasty as the first line of defense against foreign invasions. The earliest foundations of some of these walls are older than the Qin.
Ksyrie at the English Wikipedia, CC BY-SA 3.0 <http://creativecommons.org/licenses/by-sa/3.0/>, via Wikimedia Commons; https://commons.wikimedia.org/wiki/File:GreatWallofQinDynasty.png

We remember the Qin for another grand project—the famous Terracotta Army. It's safe to say that the first emperor wanted to prolong his life and fame as much as he could. Having failed to find the elixir of life, he wanted to make the afterlife as glorious as possible for himself.[63] Several thousand baked clay soldiers were found buried together with the first emperor. The soldiers must have been made with a variety of molds, but it would be an overstatement to say that each and every one of them is unique. Rather, the craftsmen must have devised a system of making a number of different soldiers by varying a set of fixed characteristics.

---

[63] Fiskesjö, Magnus. "Terra-cotta Conquest: The First Emperor's Clay Army's Blockbuster Tour of the World." p. 166

The famous Terracotta Army of the First Emperor located in the mausoleum of the first emperor, modern-day Shaanxi province.
Zossolino, CC BY-SA 4.0 <https://creativecommons.org/licenses/by-sa/4.0>, via Wikimedia Commons; https://commons.wikimedia.org/wiki/File:2015-09-22-081415_-_Terrakotta-Armee,_Grosse_Halle.jpg

A Terracotta soldier. Note the close attention to detail, especially considering the number of unearthed soldiers.
Shankar S. from Dubai, United Arab Emirates, CC BY 2.0 <https://creativecommons.org/licenses/by/2.0>, via Wikimedia Commons; https://commons.wikimedia.org/wiki/File:I_was_impressed_with_the_life-like_expression_(35300697030).jpg

A bronze chariot also found in the mausoleum of the first emperor.
Zossolino, CC BY-SA 4.0 <https://creativecommons.org/licenses/by-sa/4.0>, via Wikimedia Commons; https://commons.wikimedia.org/wiki/File:2015-09-22-091227_-_Museum_der_Grabanlage_des_Qin_Shi_Huangdi.jpg

The tomb itself is complex and illustrious, a perfect eulogy for the mighty emperor. The emperor was buried with a number of real-world companions. Sima Qian talks about the tomb and mentions that it was filled with dangerous traps for intruders. Reportedly, there was a large body of mercury hidden somewhere in the tomb, waiting for intruders. Interestingly, there are no mentions of the terracotta soldiers, not in Sima Qian's or in other texts. It is for this reason that we cannot accept that all the terracotta soldiers were made by Emperor Shi Huangdi. Of course, we wouldn't go as far as to state that they are fake or anything like that, but there should be a degree of objective criticism with respect to this fascinating archaeological find, just as there should be with any archaeological find.

Chapter 14: The End of Feudalism

As Legalism became the basis of the Qin dynasty, the end of Feudalism inevitably happened. No longer were neighboring states seen as somewhat independent vassals; they became integral parts of the first Chinese empire. In other words, the unity of the state was of the utmost importance; there was no space for divisions or dissenting voices.[64] The importance of a supreme ruler grew more and more. The Legalists believed that it was impossible for a humane leader to enforce laws and build a harmonious society. The people needed a strong hand, someone who would enforce laws cruelly and indefatigably. This all seems good on paper, but as we've seen, the Qin Empire dissolved very quickly. Even during its short reign, there were uprisings that were suffocated by ruthless power.

Some Confucian values were demonized and considered as subverting the interest of the monarch and his empire. Charity, philanthropy, rhetoric, and art were frowned upon as giving rise to dissenting voices. These practices had the potential to free people's spirits and result in an open rebellion against the emperor.

In turn, the severity of reprimands and punishments grew, even for what we may consider minor offenses. But the laws were the cruelest toward acts perceived as rebellious or in some way endangered the state's unity or the emperor's authority. For such offenses, capital punishments

---

[64] Kulmar, Tarmo, et al. "On the nature of the governing system of the Qin Empire in ancient China." p.168

were common, and they were often executed in an abominable way. People were torn and cut to pieces, their bones broken, or buried alive, to mention just a few of their ingenious yet cruel methods. Additionally, forced labor was widely used as a punishment; for instance, people could be sent to build the Great Wall. Mutilations were common as well, as numerous people had their noses or ears cut off. They could also be branded like cattle or blinded.

All these measures seemed to have been necessary to establish the emperor's authority. Because of the Warring States Period, the Legalists believed that a strong leader needed a weak populace. The imperial regime introduced so-called "joint" or "collective" responsibility. Namely, the offenses of a single person were extended to his family, who were also punished for the crime. In rural areas, several households and families were involved in this cruel circle of joint responsibility. The aristocracy wasn't free of this kind of joint responsibility, and unlike the peasants, whom the state could hardly surveil in an efficient fashion, the aristocracy was carefully monitored. All signs of disloyalty were swiftly suppressed. A new division of territory was introduced that would serve as the basis for the administration of later empires. The Qin Empire was divided into commanderies, counties, and municipalities/townships. The new administrative regions of the empire allowed for more centralized control over subjugated areas and less influence from traditional regional powers. People were appointed as heads of commanderies or counties due to their merit and reputation with the centralized administration, and their powers weren't hereditary.

We can establish certain parallels between this fairly short episode in China's history and some later periods, especially the Cultural Revolution and Mao Zedong's rule.[65] Cruelty, paranoia, and absolute loyalty to the monarch. There was no space for free debate. And this leads us to one of the most powerful and shameful instruments in the arsenal of dictators: the destruction of intellectuals and their works.

---

[65] Mao's dictatorship is one such period that comes to mind.

Chapter 15: The Burning of Books and the Burying of Scholars

Confucians and Legalists were very much two worlds apart. Although they had similar attitudes toward the importance of the monarch and the necessity of establishing authority, they disagreed on just about everything else. The Confucians were proponents of a much milder style of governance, one that was benevolent to the populace. The monarch's supremacy was an important element in the Confucian intellectual world, but his supremacy was counterweighted by the king's immaculate virtues. The populace was also expected to follow a similar path as the king, which would help improve the state by ensuring the average person was good, thoughtful, and virtuous.

The Legalists sharply disagreed with Confucians when it came to these ideas. The Legalists likely regarded the Confucians as esoteric philosophers who only roused the youth and undermined the authority of the state and the emperor.[66] The clash between the two schools of thought was inevitable, and in 213 BCE, things came to a head when Confucian books were burned and destroyed.[67]

---

[66] Confucius experienced similar difficulties during his lifetime, although he died in old age and probably of natural causes. However, the parallel between Confucius and Socrates can be seen in what happened to the followers of Confucius, as they were persecuted and executed during the Qin period.

[67] Kulmar, Tarmo, et al. "On the nature of the governing system of the Qin Empire in ancient

Officials and bureaucrats were carefully scrutinized. Anyone who openly stated that life was better in the pre-empire days could be executed, as well as those who didn't report a crime they knew about.

This crackdown on Confucians is sometimes referred to as the "Burying of Scholars," and the expression isn't metaphorical—around 460 Confucians were indeed buried alive. Confucians were also sent to build the Great Wall. Interestingly, it seems that only those who continued to talk about politics and religion were punished. Confucians who focused more on science weren't the regime's primary targets.

The political works of Confucianism weren't the only texts to be destroyed. Li Si, the man behind the regime, understood the importance of history for the neighboring states and their identity. It is for this reason that numerous ancient records of other states were destroyed to prevent the rise of separatist tendencies and ensure a more circumscribed form of patriotism.

Li Si was also behind what we would refer to today as the emperor's cult of personality. The state made sure that the populace received news about the emperor's impeccable and divine nature. Numerous inscriptions from the period were found. Here is one example:

"The emperor was a wise and prudent ruler, who worked from early morning till late night for the good of his people; all men and women were law-abiding, and everyone fulfilled their duties; there was peace and order in the empire."

Some reports ascribe superhuman reading powers to the emperor (Qin Shi Huangdi), who is said to have been able to read thirty kilograms (sixty-six pounds) of manuscripts every day. Qin Shi Huangdi probably became somewhat paranoid as the end of his life approached. As is often the case with overly powerful leaders, their desire for power often transforms into a powerful paranoia. For instance, Qin Shi Huangdi had numerous palaces near the capital to which he could move whenever he decided to do so. It is said that not even his closest companions knew about his whereabouts, which were kept secret; needless to say, some people knew about the emperor's location, and if they had let their tongues loose, they would have been executed.

The most important markers of the Qin rule are also the most important causes of its downfall. The cruelty of the Qin regime caused

---

China." p. 174

the aristocracy of various states and the rural population to rebel. Moreover, instead of focusing on coming up with a cultural style that would unify all the different states, the empire focused more on the suppression of cultures perceived to be a threat to the regime. Both the first and second emperors were too cruel, too much within their own "bubble," and unable to hear the wise voices of the aristocracy and the populace. A regime's inability to juggle the power of the monarch, the power of the few, and the power of the many, as Polybius put it many years ago, destroyed many regimes. This inability was certainly behind the fall of the Qin.

PART FIVE: THE HAN DYNASTY (206 BCE–220 CE)

Chapter 16: Rise of the Han Dynasty

After the Qin dynasty fell, someone had to step in and stop another Warring States Period from wrapping China in centuries of war. China actually witnessed another, albeit much shorter, period of civil war. The war was fought primarily between two important leaders of the rebellion against the Qin: Liu Bang and Xiang Yu.[68]

Xiang Yu emerged as the supreme leader of the rebellion against the Qin and was seemingly the one to make decisions about how the Chinese states would coexist after the first empire was dismantled. He was subsequently remembered as a great leader and entered Chinese culture through numerous stories, legends, and operas.[69] He was a very powerful leader and came from the state of Chu.

After the Qin fell in 206 BCE, Xiang Yu started materializing his plan to divide what had been the Qin dynasty into a number of smaller states in a similar way to how China looked before the Qin prevailed. This plan, which did not stay in effect for long, is sometimes referred to as Eighteen Kingdoms. However, contentions broke out again, with war once again setting its foot firmly in China.

---

[68] Zhou, Minhwa, and Meihwa Zhou. "Wisdom and Strategy— An Example for Zhang Liang and Liu Bang." In 7th International Conference on Humanities and Social Science Research (ICHSSR 2021), pp. 941-943. Atlantis Press, 2021.

[69] Chen, Pauline. "History Lessons." *New York Times*, 1993.

One of the most important leaders of this new rebellion was Liu Bang. This man must have been a fearless and incredibly authoritative war leader in a similar way to Xiang Yu. But unlike Xiang Yu, Liu Bang had fairly humble beginnings. He was born far from the aristocratic homes, although when he eventually became the emperor, numerous stories about his divine origins were made up. Liu Bang initially worked for the Qin regime in his native Chu state as a sort of pavilion chief; in other words, he was a minor official. As the Qin regime weakened, Liu Bang understood what was happening and started organizing forces against the Qin in his jurisdiction. Slowly but steadily, his influence and war prowess grew, and stories about the incredible Liu Bang started to circle. Finally, he became the king of one of the eighteen states that were formed after the fall of the Qin, specifically the state of Han. In this state, Liu Bang would muster his forces and deal one final blow to Xiang Yu.

The Feast That Almost Killed Liu Bang

But prior to open animosities between Xiang Yu and Liu Bang, there was a curious event that almost saw Liu Bang dead—the so-called "Feast at Swan Goose Gate." After the Qin were defeated in their own capital, Xianyang, a large body of forces assembled outside the capital to celebrate the victory. By this time, there was already a certain degree of tension between Liu Bang and Xiang Yu. Namely, Liu Bang was the first to arrive in Guanzhong (a region in modern-day Shaanxi province) and the first to besiege Xianyang, which is found in this region. This was taken as a sign of Liu Bang's supremacy; in fact, there seems to have been a kind of "race to Guanzhong," and the winner would become the king of Guanzhong and, thus, the king of China.

In reality, Liu Bang was the first to arrive. When other forces, including those of Xiang Yu, arrived, a great feast started. But Xiang Yu had already made his decision about Liu Bang, whom he regarded as someone who ruined his chance of being the first to take Xianyang. Through a chain of informants, Liu Bang learned about Xiang Yu's wrath. However, when he received an invitation to Xiang Yu's banquet, he couldn't refuse. Prior to going to the banquet, Liu Bang sent messages to Xiang Yu, trying to tell the latter that he wasn't trying to declare himself the ruler of China.

Liu Bang, probably against the advice of his close associates, went to pay his respects to Xiang Yu. The seating arrangement and the whole tone of the banquet were carefully constructed to put Liu Bang in a subordinate role to Xiang Yu. Moreover, it's possible that Xiang Yu and his associates planned to kill Liu Bang right there and then since he was virtually unprotected and far from his army.

According to a legend, when one of Xiang Yu's subordinates started performing a sword dance but was actually getting ready to kill Liu Bang, another Xiang Yu's associate, who did not know of the plot to kill Liu Bang, got in the way by trying to participate in the dance. Liu Bang's closest advisor, Zhang Liang, stormed out and found Liu Bang's general, Fan Kuai. Zhang Liang instructed Fan Kuai to burst into the banquet, which he did, much to the surprise of Xiang Yu, who admired Fan Kuai's military demeanor and his armor.

This must have changed the tone of the banquet, and Liu Bang succeeded in getting out under the pretext of having to use the bathroom. However, he still wanted to get back and at least say goodbye to Xiang Yu before going to sleep, but Zhang Liang and Fan Kuai vehemently objected to this.[70] It was agreed that Zhang Liang would stay and wait for a while before returning to the banquet to give Fan Kuai and Liu Bang time to return to their camp. In the end, Zhang Liang brought jade presents to Xiang Yu, apologizing for Liu Bang's absence, who, as Zhang Liang assured, was already rather drunk and had to get some sleep. Xiang Yu accepted the presents, but Xiang Yu's advisor, understanding that the opportunity to assassinate Liu Bang was now lost, shattered the jade presents to pieces, predicting the fall of Xiang Yu and the rise of Liu Bang.

A mural depicting the famous feast at the Swan Goose Gate. The picture dates from the Eastern Han dynasty and is more of a typical representation of Chinese feasts than an exact account of how the Swan Goose Gate feast looked like. Daunting Tomb.
https://commons.wikimedia.org/wiki/File:Mural_Painting_of_a_Banquet_Scene_from_the_Han_Dynasty_Tomb_of_Ta-hu-t%27ing.jpg

---

[70] Sima, Qian. Records of the grand historian: Han dynasty. Columbia University Press, 1993.

Open Conflict between Xiang Yu and Liu Bang

Immediately after this event, Xiang Yu, perhaps trying to affirm himself as the leader of China, sacked and burned the Qin capital, Xianyang. Interestingly, Liu Bang, who, as mentioned, arrived first at Xianyang, refrained from burning and looting. Both leaders of the rebellion had similar aspirations (to become the supreme ruler of China) but had different *modi operandi*.

After amassing a vast fortune, Xiang Yu decided to return home to the state of Chu. There, he proclaimed himself king of Chu and "promoted" the previous king of Chu (Huai) to the rank of "righteous emperor." Of course, this title was merely symbolic, and in any case, the "righteous emperor" was soon assassinated on the orders of Xiang Yu.

Roughly in the same period (206 BCE), Liu Bang started preparing for an all-out rebellion against the forces of Xiang Yu. He started slowly taking newly formed kingdoms one by one. By 205 BCE, Liu Bang had amassed a force of around 560,000 men (according to ancient historian Sima Qian) and marched eastward toward the Chu capital of Pengcheng. Since Xiang Yu was busy fighting other rebellious groups, namely the Chi in the north, Liu Bang was able to take Pengcheng with little to no resistance.[71] The soldiers were enjoying the spoils of war, namely the fortunes of Pengcheng and its beautiful women, when Xiang Yu struck back and inflicted a catastrophic defeat on Liu Bang's Han army. The Han army started a disorderly retreat, which resulted in even more casualties. During this retreat, hundreds of thousands of soldiers perished in rivers, mountains, and ambushes, as they lacked even basic necessities. Sima Qian reports that when Liu Bang's soldiers were forced into a river called the Sui, the subsequent carnage left so many corpses that they dammed up the river.

Liu Bang found himself surrounded over the course of his retreat, and the circle was getting tighter and tighter. All of a sudden, a great storm overtook the battlefield. It was so powerful that it was able to make trees fall. Dust and debris filled the air, and the day turned into night. The subsequent chaos allowed Liu Bang to break through and save his life with as little as thirty cavalrymen.

But this wasn't the only close call. You may remember that Liu Bang was actually born in the state of Chu and had family there; in fact, his

---

[71] Ibid.

children, wife, mother, and father were all living in the state of Chu when Liu Bang came to defeat Xiang Yu. So, Liu Bang wanted to save his family as he was fleeing. His children, his wife, and his parents were already fleeing, and it was by pure chance that Liu Bang came across his son (future Emperor Hui) and daughter (future Princess Yuan) on the road. However, Liu Bang's caravan was spotted by Chu cavalrymen, and the two groups engaged in what must have been an incredibly tense chase. To make the scene even more dramatic, as Sima Qian reports, Liu Bang grew extremely worried about his children making the carriage heavier, which would make it easier for the Chu horsemen to catch up with them. So, he tried to push his children out of the carriage, but fortunately, Lord Teng, one of Liu Bang's closest associates, saved his son and daughter.

Liu Bang's wife, mother, and father weren't so lucky, as they were captured by the Chu forces.

The year 204 BCE saw Liu Bang regaining control over his forces, mustering new ones, and retreating to more friendly areas. He also ensured he had a road, which was important for moving provisions. The road meandered together with the Yellow River and connected less-well-supplied areas with the grain-rich Yellow River Basin.

Xiang Yu, who was advised by Fan Tseng, did everything he could to cut off this road and make life harder for the Han. It is at this moment and under the threat of having his main cities besieged by the Chu that Liu Bang decided to start negotiating with the Chu, aiming to buy himself some time before being able to recover his forces and deal a counterblow. An envoy arrived in the Han state, and Liu Bang started to unravel his plan to sow dissent in the heart of the Chu leadership. He first bestowed the Chu negotiators a grand feast. But then, he "learned" they had been sent by Xiang Yu. (Liu Band pretended that he thought these negotiators were sent by Fan Tseng independently of Xiang Yu to sow discord between the two.) Liu Bang ordered servants to carry away the lavish meals and drinks and instead bring in a much more modest dinner.

Needless to say, the Chu negotiators were astonished at this mistreatment and were suspicious as to why Liu Bang changed his demeanor once he "learned" that the negotiators were sent by Xiang Yu. They reported this to Xiang Yu, raising his suspicions about Fan Tseng. The latter was angered by these probably unjustified suspicions. He handed in his resignation but soon died of health complications related to an ulcerous sore.

Back in Han, the situation was going from bad to worse. Liu Bang was besieged in the city of Jung-yang, and it seemed that his final capture was imminent. But Liu Bang's general, Han Xin, stepped in. Han Xin decided to lead a decoy attack disguised as the king of the Han himself, making space for the real Liu Bang to escape. In order to make this decoy attack more believable, thousands of women from the city were dressed up in battle armor and led outside through the eastern gate. While Han Xin was handing in his "royal surrender" to Xiang Yu, Liu Bang fled through the western gate with a few dozen cavalrymen. Han Xin was burned alive.

This was a fairly smart move because Liu Bang managed to escape, and the city of Jung-yang was still in the hands of the Han. The defense of the city was now the duty of Chou Ko, Lord Tsung, and Wei Pao (who was a former enemy of the Han but now an ally). Chou Ko and Lord Tsung decided to kill Wei Pao since they didn't want an ex-enemy with them. The Chu army finally prevailed and took Jung-yang; when Chou Ko was offered the place of a Chu general, he decided to choose a more glorious yet more tragic fate. Chou Ko retorted, "If you do not hurry and surrender to the king of Han, you will be taken prisoner! You are no match for him!"[72] It is not surprising that Chou Ko was then boiled alive at the orders of Xiang Yu. Lord Tsung was executed as well, although not in such a dramatic fashion.

Liu Bang's Final Victory

The year 203 BCE saw Liu Bang take part in more military campaigns. Once again, he was besieged in a city, this time Cheng-kao. However, this time, he was forced to flee alone. After this, he was able to organize his forces and, most importantly, further cooperate with his allies, who were attacking the Chu and making it harder for the Chu to focus on destroying the Han. The forces of Peng Yueh were especially a nuisance to the Chu supply lines; they were also able to foment rebellion in Chu-controlled regions, such as the Liang region. Enraged by years of what seemed to be unsuccessful warfare against Liu Bang, Xiang Yu decided to boil Bang's father alive if Liu Bang didn't surrender immediately. Liu Bang's response, to say the least, was incredible:

---

[72] Ibid.

"When you and I bowed together before King Huai and acknowledged our allegiance to him, we took a vow to be brothers. Therefore my father is your father, too. If you insist now upon boiling your own father, I hope you will be good enough to send me a cup of the soup!"[73]

Hsiang Po, Xiang Yu's new advisor, was against this drastic move, and Hsiang argued that boiling the old man alive would be futile since Liu Bang obviously didn't care about it, claiming the only thing he wanted was to rule the world. What then ensued was a fairly stable stalemate, with both sides making no notable moves. Xiang Yu, who was known for his valor and physical prowess, decided to challenge Liu Bang to a personal duel, just the two of them. Liu Bang was possibly aware that the odds were in Xiang Yu's favor, so he didn't agree to a duel.

Xiang Yu started sending his strongest and bravest men to challenge the bravest Han men to battle. There was a highly skilled horseback archer within the Han ranks who came from a barbarian tribe (Loufan) that lived close to the "civilized" Chinese world. This horse archer killed three of Yu's challengers. Xiang Yu was once again enraged and approached Cheng Kao, the city where Liu Bang and his forces were stationed, and challenged the Loufan horseback archer. It is said that the spectacle and incredible scream of Xiang Yu distressed the Loufan archer so much that he fled back to the city.

Liu Bang, having learned about this strange occasion, decided to leave the city and talk to Xiang Yu at a safe distance. Once again expressing his desire not to fight the much stronger Xiang Yu, the leader of Chu grew extremely frustrated and drew out a concealed crossbow, wounding Liu Bang, who fled back into the city.

More hostilities continued. The Han allies continued harassing the Chu, and Xiang Yu was forced to leave his generals to besiege Cheng Kao and Liu Bang, marching eastward to help fight the Han allies. One of the most important instructions to his generals was something along the lines of "Stay put, don't pitch battles, and don't fight battles when Liu Bang challenges you." After a few days of taunting and mocking, the Chu forces were led into battle by General Tsao Chiu. In order to meet Liu Bang's forces, the Chu forces had to cross the river Ssu. Liu Bang attacked them just as they were crossing the river, massacring the Chu

---

[73] Ibid.

men.

This was one of the turning points of the war. Xiang Yu was forced to march back and face Liu Bang's army, even though his own men were exhausted. Another round of negotiations was held. Xiang Yu offered the lives of Liu Bang's wife, father, and mother and a partition of Chinese lands. Liu Bang acquiesced. But Zhang Liang, Bang's closest advisor, saw an opportunity for a complete victory over the Chu. Zhang Liang argued that the Chu were exhausted and had almost no allies. The Han, on the other hand, had plenty of supplies and a lot of allies on their side. Now was the time to attack!

Liu Bang listened to this wise counsel and attacked the Chu in 202 BCE. However, he once again suffered a crushing defeat since his closest allies, Peng Yueh and Han Hsin, did not show up at the agreed time. Once again, the good counsel of Zhang Liang came to Liu's rescue. As Zhang Liang argued, both Peng Yueh and Han Hsin were unhappy since they had already done a lot for Liu Bang without receiving any territorial gains. If they received land, they would be more motivated to help Bang end this long war.

After receiving territorial grants, the allies continued their operation, and the circle around Xiang Yu grew smaller and smaller. His camp was encircled by the enemy, his provisions were thin, and morale was low. After hearing the sounds of Chu songs coming from the enemy camp, Xiang Yu understood that many of his men had joined the enemy's ranks. Saying his last farewell to his concubine, the beautiful Lady Yu, Xiang Yu drove out of the camp and broke the encirclement, along with a few hundred horsemen. But the group lost the way and was pursued by the Han horsemen. Realizing that everything had been lost and that the worthiest thing would be to make one last stand, Xiang Yu divided his men into several groups and ordered them to inflict as much damage as possible on the enemy. Xiang Yu is said to have slain up to one hundred men on his own.

He managed to break out and reach the Yangtze River with a few fellow soldiers. A village head offered to take them to the other side. Xiang Yu firmly believed that the heavens themselves wanted to take him down and bring Liu Bang to power and had already decided on how he would end his life. He wasn't going to try to flee as far as he could. Instead, he gave his beloved horse to the kind village head and returned to face the Han soldiers one last time. Once again, Sima Qian tells us that Xiang Yu killed hundreds of Han soldiers, suffering bitter wounds himself. Then, he spotted Liu Bang's cavalry commander, Lu Matung, and his entourage. Even in his last moments, Xiang Yu kept his honor and pride, saying, "I have heard that Han has offered a reward of a thousand catties of gold and a fief of ten thousand households for my head. I will do you the favor!"[74]

The Han soldiers then literally battled for Xiang Yu's body and head. The victors of this unworthy scuffle divided the rewards quite literally as they dismembered Xiang Yu's body. His death marked the end of a period of calamity, which had lasted ever since the Qin were overthrown some five years before. In 202 BCE, the Han, heralded by Liu Bang, finally gained supremacy over the whole of the Chinese civilized world. Liu Bang wasn't overly cruel when it came to finalizing his ascent to power. Namely, he spared the state of Lu, Xiang Yu's native state, and Xiang Yu's family.

The Han Emperor

Liu Bang, later known as Emperor Gaozu, is an incredibly interesting personality, so this short excerpt on him won't do him justice. Still, we'll try to sketch him as a person and lay out his most important achievements as emperor.

There are many poetic stories about Liu Bang's early life, and quite a lot of them firmly step into the mythical, legendary, or purely superstitious realms. For instance, Liu Bang's mother, Dame Liu, is said to have met a god prior to giving birth to her prodigal son. His father, who was looking for Dame Liu, eventually found her but saw a large dragon hovering over his wife. Dame Liu conceived Liu Bang after this event. Liu Bang is said to have had seventy-two moles on his left leg, and this number might have been a magical number since it's the product of two equally magical numbers in Chinese culture: eight and nine.

When the time came, Liu Bang passed an official exam and became the village head of the Ssu River region. Sometime around this period, Liu Bang showed his love of women and wine, often visiting brothels in his town. Sima Qian even mentions the poetic names of these places, such as Dame Wang's or old lady Wu's place. Liu Bang wasn't exactly a good customer, as he often drank and enjoyed the services of the ladies on credit. However, Liu Bang's prodigality once again stepped in. Even

---

[74] Ibid.

though he rarely paid, he had a sort of lucky allure with him; every time he came, the brothel's profits increased! What's more, when Liu Bang was exhausted from pleasure and fell asleep, people could notice a sort of dragon hovering over him.[75]

Then, there are stories about people "reading" great future deeds from the faces of Liu Bang and his family. In fact, this was how Liu Bang was married to his first wife, Lady Lu, who became Empress Lu. Her father, Master Lu, noticed that there was something great about Liu Bang, even though the latter was a simple village head. He decided to marry his daughter to Liu Bang. Later, when an elderly man was passing through Liu Bang's village, he saw Liu Bang's wife, son, and daughter, and he predicted a glorious future for all of them just by reading their faces.

It's certain that Liu Bang was an extraordinary man. Curiously, however, he wasn't an exceptional statesman or a worthy general. His talent lay elsewhere—he knew how to recognize talented and able individuals who could do the job and remain loyal to him. In fact, Liu Bang himself emphasized that he could not compare with Zhang Liang's strategic mind, nor could he measure up to Xiao He's ability as a statesman. However, Liu Bang knew how to control powerful individuals, and it's due to this ability that he ultimately conceived a powerful Chinese empire.[76]

But let's leave these stories now and rejoin our emperor where we left him, at the very start of his reign. In the year 202 BCE and after the death of Xiang Yu, Emperor Gaozu still had a lot of work to do to affirm himself as the great emperor of China. There were some revolts that needed to be quenched, and Gaozu also had to appoint the proper men as (nominal) heads of state. In 201 BCE, Liu Fei, the emperor's son, became the governor of the state of Qi. In 200 BCE, more revolts needed to be pacified, but the capital of the new empire was completed. It was called Chang-an (modern-day Xian, Shaanxi province) and was home to the "Palace of Lasting Joy" and infrastructure for the bureaucracy and public officials.

---

[75] Ibid.

[76] Hardy, Grant, and Anne Behnke Kinney. *The establishment of the Han empire and imperial China*. Greenwood Publishing Group, 2005.

Chapter 17: Western and Eastern Han Dynasties

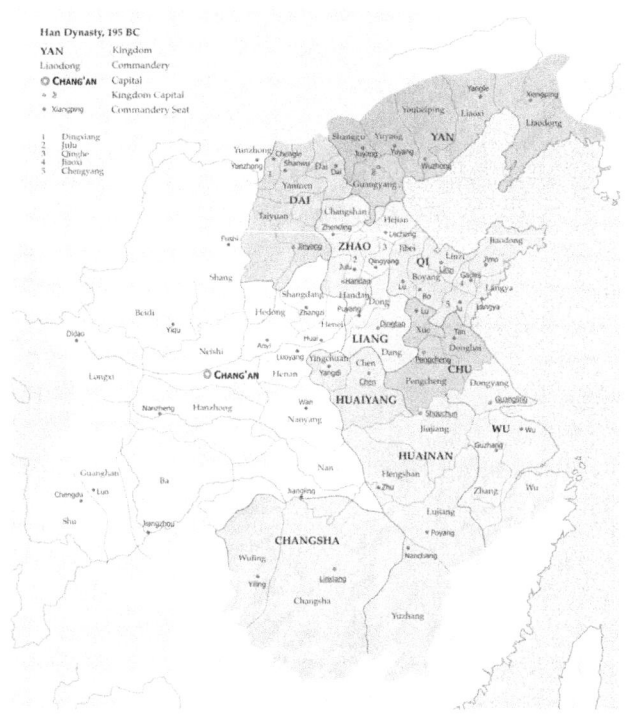

Early Western Han state.
Esiymbro, CC BY-SA 4.0 <https://creativecommons.org/licenses/by-sa/4.0>, via Wikimedia Commons; https://commons.wikimedia.org/wiki/File:Han_dynasty_Kingdoms_195_BC.png

Emperor Gaozu established a stable dynasty that ruled China for centuries to come (albeit with some breaks). Emperor Gaozu died in 195 BCE, leaving the throne to his young son, Lui Fei (Emperor Hui), who was only fifteen years old when his father died. So Gaozu's wife, Empress Lu, stepped in and served as regent. Empress Lu furthered the interests of her own clan, giving numerous members of her family important posts. Emperor Hui died of an illness in 188 BCE, which allowed Empress Lu to increase her influence even further. Two alleged sons of Emperor Hui, Liu Gong and Liu Hong, then became emperors. Both were very young and easily manipulated.

It's clear that Empress Lu tried to establish herself as the supreme ruler, but owing to the rules of the time, she could only be the regent of "real" emperors.

Empress Lu wasn't a bad ruler, but she did try to increase the influence of her own clan at the expense of Emperor Gaozu's clan. It is for this reason that after her death in 180 BCE, influential members of the Lu clan were massacred, and the supremacy of Liu Bang's clan was assured once again, this time thanks to Emperor Wen, who was one of the numerous sons Liu Bang had with his consorts.

The following forty years, during which time Emperor Wen (180-157 BCE) and his son Emperor Jing (157-141 BCE) ruled, were remembered as relatively peaceful and prosperous. During this period, the reach and power of the central government were further increased, and the power and influence of provincial kings were curbed. The influence of nobles also decreased, as the state would take over their possessions if they died without an heir or if they broke the law.

Next came Emperor Wu, who reigned between 141 and 87 BCE. His reign was also known for being peaceful, stable, and prosperous. The empire was expanded and protected by building the Great Wall, which helped stop the invasions of the northern barbarians. Emperor Wu is also presented in literature as the emperor who finally allowed an all-encompassing adoption of Confucianism in the court and government, although he did not outright reject the Legalist tradition.

During the long reign of Emperor Wu, Chinese astronomy became very important. First of all, one has to keep in mind the close relationship between philosophy, science, and myth in the ancient age. Specialization is a relatively modern thing, and erudition was much more common in ancient times (both in Europe and China, as well as elsewhere). So, intellectuals close to the court were well versed in practically all fields of knowledge, and astronomy/astrology was an important part of what Emperor Wu expected from his intellectuals. Back then, the observation of stars wasn't simply a scientific act. In the case of Emperor Wu, astronomy/astrology provided a way to inquire about the future and establish contact between people and higher entities. There was another, very specific goal as well: ensuring the emperor's immortality.[77]

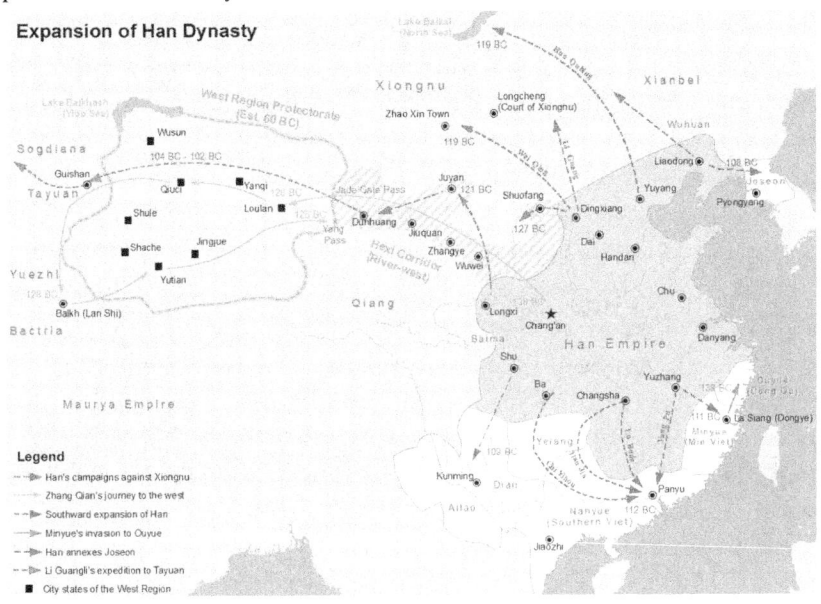

Expansion of the Han toward the north, south, and west during the reign of Emperor Wu. This would be the basis for subsequent contact between Chinese and faraway Asian and European civilizations.
SY, CC BY-SA 4.0 <https://creativecommons.org/licenses/by-sa/4.0>, via Wikimedia Commons; https://commons.wikimedia.org/wiki/File:Han_Expansion.png

It is somewhat ironic that a crucial incentive for the development of Chinese astronomy came as a result of the emperor's superstition. For instance, it's said that Emperor Wu once encountered a man who claimed to be hundreds of years old and who allegedly held the secret to eternal youth. This man was able to strike at the emperor's vanity and vivid imagination. He succeeded, like many who came after him, to

---

[77] Cullen, Christopher. "Motivations for Scientific Change in Ancient China: Emperor Wu and the Grand Inception Astronomical Reforms of 104 BC." *Journal for the History of Astronomy* 24, no. 3 (1993): 185-203.

profit by telling fantastic stories to Emperor Wu. Unfortunately, the emperor wasn't really that gullible, and he would see through these people's attempts to fool him by planting fake evidence and things like that. Everyone who was caught doing so or anyone with fake prophecies risked execution.

Emperor Wu was also obsessed with the mythical Yellow Emperor and started believing in stories of people who drew parallels between his reign and that of the Yellow Emperor.[78] In myth, the Yellow Emperor is a being that existed (or continued to exist spiritually during the times of Emperor Wu) in the intersection between the earthly and the divine. It's possible that the Yellow Emperor originated from Shang deities and has been translated into a real historical person over the course of time. Then, during the Qin dynasty, and especially thanks to Qin Shi Huangdi's megalomania, the myth of a Yellow Emperor who was also a god was once again revived. In fact, the "di" from Huangdi was commonly used to denote the qualities of a god.

One of these parallels between the Yellow Emperor and Emperor Wu was closely tied to astronomy and the Chinese calendar. Namely, some people claimed that such an ancient "holiday" during the reign of Emperor Wu fell on the same day as during the reign of the Yellow Emperor. In other words, the emperor's "need" to have good astronomers in the court came from his desire to relive the example of the Yellow Emperor.

Emperor Wu's ambitions, capabilities, and long reign resulted in the significant territorial expansion of China, especially westward. The vast, unexplored, and sparsely populated steppe highlands must have seemed alluring to Emperor Wu, who wanted to project his power as far as possible. Beginning in the times of Emperor Wu, the Chinese had considered the modern-day Xinjiang region (a very large central Asian region in the far west of China, bordering countries like Kazakhstan, Kyrgyzstan, and Tajikistan) as their sphere of influence. This was more of an exploratory expedition, and the primary goal was to establish diplomatic relations with whomever the Chinese explorers came across. And they came across the likes of the Dayuan and Kangju people, who inhabited the modern-day regions of Uzbekistan and Tajikistan.

---

[78] Ibid.

The steppes might have been a simpler feat compared to Wu's southern conquests. During Emperor Wu's reign, Xinjiang and modern-day southern China came under the influence of the Han Empire. Provinces like Fujian, Guangdong, or Guanxi wouldn't have been within modern-day China if it hadn't been for Emperor Wu's southern excursions. To do this, Wu's army first had to defeat the states of Minyue and Nanyue.

Finally, Emperor Wu sorted out the problem of northern invaders by becoming the invading force. The Xiongnu group of nomadic tribes was the primary target. The Chinese civilization was threatened for centuries before and after by these tribes since they were drawn southward by the rich cities of China.

It is not an uncommon occurrence in history that after a particularly strong and authoritative leader comes a period of calamity and chaos. It didn't take long for China to enter such a period after Emperor Wu died in 87 BCE, although this time, things didn't end in centuries of civil wars. Emperor Wu's youngest son, Zhao, came to the throne, and during his reign, which ended in 74 BCE with his untimely death (he was only twenty years old), the power was essentially in the hands of Huo Gang, an important official under Emperor Wu.[79] Emperor Zhao didn't have a son who would inherit the throne, so Huo Gang first chose Liu He, Emperor Wu's grandson, as the heir. Liu He must have done something wrong since he was deposed after just about twenty days, and Wu's great-grandson, Emperor Xuan, came to the throne.[80] He was also chosen by Huo Gang. Huo Gang's final choice turned out to be for the better since Emperor Xuan's reign was known for its stability and prosperity. For some time, Huo Gang continued to be a close advisor to the emperor in spite of his intention to step down. Some good things happened during the reign of Emperor Xuan; for instance, he issued important reforms to the judicial system, which moderated the harshness of judges and made appeals easier. Meritocracy was at its height, with able people finding their way to the top offices. The emperor was also a friend of the arts, with numerous poets and literary workers being supported directly by the court. Emperor Xuan died in 48 BCE, and his son, Emperor Yuan, took

---

[79] Dreyer, Edward L. "Zhao Chongguo: A Professional Soldier of China's Former Han Dynasty." *The Journal of Military History* 72, no. 3 (2008): 665-725.

[80] Gao, Jiyi. "Emperor Xuan, Emperor Zhang and the Rise and Decline of Zhangju in the Han Dynasty." Hanxue Yanjiu (Chinese Studies) 25, no. 1 (2007).

over.

Up until then, the Chinese empire remained fairly prosperous. Even during the times of Emperor Yuan and the subsequent domination of his wife, Empress Wang, China was fairly stable. Her influence increased after Emperor Yuan died in 33 BCE. A number of emperors sat on the throne, but Empress Wang, who became dowager empress, remained very influential and increased the influence of her own Wang clan.[81] This was possibly the main thing that pushed China back into chaos. Relatives of Empress Wang grew stronger and stronger, and it's entirely unsurprising that Wang Mang decided to depose the young and insignificant Emperor Ping and replace him with the even younger Ruzi Ying, who was formally in power from 6 to 9 CE. Eventually, Wang Mang decided to stop pretending and declared himself the first emperor of a new dynasty, the Xin.[82]

It is not possible here to dissect all the events that led to the short-lived Xin dynasty and the short-lived chaos that came soon after Wang Mang rose to the throne. Suffice it to say that this was a natural consequence of the Chinese political dynamics at the time, with ruthlessness, mischievousness, and insidiousness being equally important as political wisdom and real merit. Wang Mang wasn't necessarily going to be a bad emperor, and there are some indications that he had grand plans for China. But ultimately, his usurpation of the Han dynasty led to a civil war and the formation of a very peculiar group called the Red Eyebrows.

Wang Mang was also unlucky. Right when he was working hard to implement his grandiose reforms, there was a great flood in China that left a lot of farmers without much food. A revolt was unavoidable, and the Red Eyebrows and other groups finally sacked the capital of the Western Han, Chang'an, in 23 CE. Together with other groups of rebels, the Red Eyebrows chose a new emperor who was related to the Han named Gengshi. He didn't rule for long, as the Red Eyebrows overthrew him and placed a child whom they could more easily control. Finally, they were defeated by the founder of the Eastern Han, Emperor

---

[81] Xiong, Victor Cunrui, and Kenneth James Hammond, eds. Routledge Handbook of Imperial Chinese History. Routledge, 2019. p. 25-38.

[82] L'Haridon, Béatrice. "WANG MANG 王莽 (c. 45 BCE–23 CE) AND CLASSICAL LEARNING AS PATH TO SUPREME POWER." *Early China* 45 (2022): 51-72.

Guangwu, who chose a new capital city, Luoyang. Since Emperor Guangwu was related to the Western Han, he had the leverage needed to help him crush the rebels who were increasingly seeking to satisfy their own needs as opposed to the needs of the Chinese civilization.

Chapter 18: Cultural and Military Developments

Administrative Reforms

The foundations for the empire were partially inherited from older empires and partially laid by Liu Bang and his important officials. We already mentioned Zhang Liang, whose advice was crucial in the period of the establishment of the Han dynasty. Zhang Liang was more of a Sun Tzu type of advisor, aiding Liu Bang in politico-strategic decision-making. But there were other important advisors, such as Xiao He (or Ho), who focused more on law and administration. Xiao He became Emperor Gaozu's chancellor and was instrumental in the legal, cultural, and administrative improvements related to the early Han period. Even before 202 BCE and the final victory of the Han, Xiao He was very active, governing vast areas while Liu Bang was waging war. During this challenging period, Xiao He was tasked with simplifying laws, setting up district offices, and spreading Han propaganda and dynastic temples.

In 202 BCE, Xiao He was bestowed with the highest possible merits by Emperor Gaozu. Xiao He had so many privileges that other officials became envious, and the emperor had to remind everyone that it was Xiao He who had practically governed the whole empire for years. Under the guidance of Xiao He and other important officials, the Legalist tradition, which was characteristic of the Qin empire, was slowly augmented with the suppressed Confucian tradition.[83] Xiao He is also credited with the establishment of the Han code. Apart from being a great organizer and administrator, Xiao He was also a great connoisseur of the law. He took the existing Qin code, revised it, and quite possibly made it more humane.[84] His code consisted of nine chapters, with statutes on robbery and theft, arrest, dereliction, stables, and much else. It was a fairly complex code that was more attuned to the contemporary situation and most certainly more conducive to peace and stability in comparison to the old Qin code.

The early Han dynasty had an elaborate taxation system, which included both grain and labor. Provincial chiefs—so-called "kings" who were appointed directly by Emperor Gaozu—were instrumental in tax collection, defense from external enemies, and execution of laws. The empire itself was initially divided into thirds, with the eastern kingdoms (ten of them) constituting two-thirds of the empire. The western third of the country was divided into provinces or commanderies that were under the direct control of the central government. Initially, the "kingdoms" in the east were granted to numerous allies of Liu Bang. But many of these chiefs soon revolted against Emperor Gaozu, and fairly quickly, the emperor was forced to appoint people closer to him, usually his family members, as provincial chiefs.

The emperor also brought order to the nobility. Namely, Gaozu divided the elite into twenty distinct "levels" of nobility. Purportedly, the basic assumption of the new nobility was a meritocracy, and it's probable that this rule was enforced to a certain extent. Furthermore, the emperor appointed 150 marquises, the only hereditary noble title (excluding the imperial family) that could be passed directly to children. It goes without saying that noble children were given a chance to deserve higher positions, and many of them took that chance.

As far as the central government is concerned, it was separated into three government sectors: the civil service, military, and internal investigation service (usually tasked with monitoring the elites and spying on officials). On the local level, this division was more or less preserved,

---

[83] Dubs, Homer H. "The victory of Han Confucianism." *Journal of the American Oriental Society* 58, no. 3 (1938): 435-449.

[84] Xueqin, Li, and Xing Wen. "New light on the Early-Han code: a reappraisal of the Zhangjiashan bamboo-slip legal texts." *Asia Major* (2001): 125-146.

so there were county military and civil authorities as separate branches. A very important office was the county magistrate, who was, in essence, the civil representative of the central government. County magistrates had a very important mixture of powers. First of all, they were responsible for the collection of taxes, even though they didn't collect them personally. Next, they had both executive and judicial powers, meaning they were in charge of arrests but also judging and sentencing criminals. They were also in charge of infrastructure maintenance, specifically the maintenance of waterways.

County magistrates were supreme judges in their respective counties, so they also resolved civil disputes between individuals and were in charge of applying the central government's agenda when it came to, for instance, agricultural planning. To top it all off, they were in charge of the census, which means they assessed the size of the population in their county, the people's total possessions, etc.

County magistrates couldn't serve in their native counties, which must have been a way for the central government to reduce corruption and nepotism. Moreover, their salary was paid by the central government, and the pay was based on their job performance. County magistrates were closely monitored and had to send periodic reports on the state of things in their county to the central government.

Confucianism Came Back!

Besides this careful planning of state administration, there's another reason the Han dynasty functioned effectively and efficiently: Confucianism. You may remember that Confucianism was considered the most bitter enemy of the Qin. We may argue that their failure to understand the importance of Confucianism is one of the reasons for the Qin dynasty's downfall. The Han didn't repeat this mistake. However, if it was only up to Liu Bang, Confucianism might have remained underground. Initially, Liu Bang had a particular disdain for Confucian scholars. It is said that Liu Bang, who was a fairly simple and robust man, once encountered a Confucian scholar. He took off the man's cap and urinated in it![85]

Fortunately for his successors and the whole of China, Emperor Gaozu learned to appreciate Confucians, albeit not without nudges from

---

[85] Hardy, Grant, and Anne Behnke Kinney. *The establishment of the Han empire and imperial China*. Greenwood Publishing Group, 2005.

officials who were aware that years of warfare must have molded Liu Bang into a strict, no-nonsense, in-your-face type of person. The following nudge from an official pointed out in a very visual way why Liu Bang's old style of administration had to be adapted to suit the needs of the empire: "You may have won the world on horseback, but can you rule it on horseback?"[86]

However, Confucianism didn't become the official "religion" until sometime later. It wasn't the only creed or philosophical outlook. As we've seen, the Han took a lot from the Qin, such as their legal code and the essence of the Legalist tradition. But unlike the Qin, the Han knew how to combine Legalism and Confucianism (and other viewpoints), building a firm, authoritative government that wasn't too severe.

Confucian ethics and focus on ancient ceremonies provided an important cultural boost to Chinese elites and officials. The ancient ceremonies and rituals brought order to relationships between the imperial family and the elites, affirming the emperor's place within his own empire.

All these and other cultural developments had very palpable results. For instance, Xu Shen, an important Chinese scholar who lived in the 1st and 2nd centuries CE, composed the first Chinese dictionary around 100 CE.[87] This dictionary focuses on the graphic etymology of Chinese characters. The dictionary (often referred to as *Shuowen Jiezi*) shows the development of Chinese culture; reflecting on the language people use every day is no small intellectual feat.

Sima Qian has already been mentioned; this intellectual was instrumental in the development of Chinese historiography. His objective treatment of incredibly complex historical events spanning centuries still stands as a shining example of how historiographers should think about past times. Sima Qian was regarded by subsequent annalists as a "true" historian and the father of Chinese historiography. It is true that Sima Qian's father was also a revered annalist and that Sima Qian's writings bear marks of his own day and age. Sima Qian, much in accordance with the revivified Confucian values, considered furthering the cause his father had dedicated his life to as his ultimate goal.

---

[86] Ibid.

[87] Bottéro, Françoise, and Christoph Harbsmeier. "The" Shuowen Jiezi" Dictionary and the Human Sciences in China." *Asia Major* (2008): 249-271.

Intellectual rigorousness and objectivity, on the one hand, and filial piety and the sense of duty, on the other, are the two main dimensions of Sima Qian's work.

Sima Qian followed the true methods of historiography. He gathered evidence when he could, and when he was in doubt, he wasn't shy about indicating it. For his passage on Confucius, he relied heavily on his personal visits to Confucius's birthplace. He also sought people who had knowledge of past events, compiling different stories and trying to come up with the most logical descriptions of events. But there's also the emotional background: Sima Tan's (Sima Qian's father) unusual position as an intellectual/astronomer/astrologist in the court of Emperor Wu. Sima Tan wasn't treated that well by Emperor Wu, who seemed to have thrown Sima Tan in the same basket as musicians and jesters. Sima Qian must have been deeply shaken by this lack of respect for his father and sought to obtain the respect he believed his family deserved.

Here, we have to remind ourselves of the importance of filial piety in Han China. A very important Confucian dictum was that "a son does not consider that he has his own self."[88] This dictum is important in explaining Sima Qian's motivation to write his books. And on a much wider scale, it shows us the Confucian version of order and peace, where everyone and everything has its own place and purpose. In a way, this trait of Chinese culture remained and has served as a major point for the creation of our modern distinction between collectivistic and individualistic cultures.

The cultural developments of Han China served as a basis for important technological and scientific breakthroughs. Paper was invented in China in the early 2nd century CE.[89] The invention is often ascribed to Cai Lun, who was the head of the government's workshops in the eastern capital of Han, Luoyang. This invention was a big breakthrough because Chinese people mainly used bamboo slips or silk instead of paper, the former being cumbersome and the latter exceedingly costly. Beginning in the 2nd century CE, the Chinese started using hemp to produce relatively cheap paper. Hemp was readily available, cheap, and relatively easy to craft into pieces of paper ready for writing. Needless to say, the Chinese people continued experimenting with paper, and many different plants

---

[88] Nylan, Michael. "Sima Qian: A True Historian?." p. 206

[89] Cartwright, Mark. Paper in Ancient China. *World History Encyclopedia*, 2017.

were used in the process.

Together with educational developments, owed primarily to the ascent of Confucianism and the opening of official schools, most importantly, the Imperial University (Taixue), the invention of paper propelled Chinese culture into a new era. It was now easier than ever before to obtain a good education (needless to say, a vast majority of people remained illiterate and uneducated). It was also easier than ever to obtain books and to actually practice writing, which, up until the invention of paper, had been very costly and thus only available to a few individuals. The education of women also progressed during the Han dynasty, although, of course, the most important lessons taught to women at this time were their manners and their role in the family.[90] The following excerpt from a correspondence between a Confucian scholar and a government official named Gongsun Hong and Emperor Wu shows the value of education and plans to further expand education early on in the Han period:

"In order to fill the offices of erudites we suggest that fifty additional students be selected and declared exempt from the usual labor services. The master of ritual shall be charged with the selection of students from among men of the people who are eighteen years of age or older and who are of good character and upright behavior in order to supply candidates for the quota of students of the erudites."[91]

The Han Army

Periods of relative peace and stability allowed for the development of vast public projects and initiatives. Conscription during the Han dynasty was fairly efficient and served three main purposes: men serving in the capital, men defending the borders of the empire, and men serving in their places of birth. Conscription was universal, and all males were supposed to serve in the capital, defend the borders, and retain law and order in their own regions. Military service started sometime around when males turned twenty.[92] It was taken seriously, and it was universal in

---

[90] Zhijie, Huo. "The significance of female education during the Han Dynasty." Вестник Бурятского государственного университета. Гуманитарные исследования Внутренней Азии 4 (2016): 54-59.

[91] Van Ess, Hans. "Emperor Wu of the Han and the First August Emperor of Qin in Sima Qian's Shiji." *Birth of an Empire* 5 (2013): 239.

[92] Ch'ien, Mu. *Merits and Demerits of Political Systems in Dynastic China*. Springer Berlin Heidelberg, 2019.

the real meaning of the word—some very high officials didn't hesitate to send their sons to serve in the military!

At any given moment, there were two large armies, with seventy thousand soldiers combined, stationed in the capital. One army, usually referred to as the South Army, was tasked with defending the imperial palace; the North Army was tasked with defending the capital itself. Serving in the capital wasn't such a bad thing, as the government covered all expenses, such as traveling to and back from the capital and food and drink, during the length of a man's service in the capital, which was around one year.

The frontier service was somewhat different. The Qin dynasty inherited a three-day frontier service from the smaller feudal states that it (forcibly) united. Before unification, a three-day frontier service functioned well since states were fairly small, and it didn't take too much time to arrive at the frontier from any place in the state. The Qin simply adopted this system, disregarding the fact that they led a much larger state. The Qin government still demanded the three-day frontier service in spite of sending men from one end of the empire to the other. It's possible that frustration concerning this particular service was one of the reasons for the fairly quick downfall of the Qin.

The Han were smarter and had a large enough administration to deal with the matter of frontier service. The service formally still lasted for only three days, but there was a possibility of paying not to serve at the frontier. So, the government amassed enough money to finance longer stays at the frontier for soldiers who were willing to do so.

Trade and Contact with Faraway Peoples

Increased security made it possible for trade to flourish further. And it wasn't only internal trade that flourished; the Chinese started establishing stable contact with Eurasian cultures. Zhang Qian, who served as a diplomat and an explorer under Emperor Wu (r. 141–87 BCE), was one of the first Chinese to explore central Asia and find new opportunities for trade and diplomatic relations. His travels to central Asia also brought modern-day Xinjiang province under China's sphere of influence. The Silk Road started to function thanks to Zhang Qian's explorations, and the concept of the bridge between China and the rest of the world continues to live today under the form of the modern Belt and Road initiative.

Because of the Parthian Empire, Chinese silk started reaching European states, and silk soon became a status symbol among Greeks and Romans. Note that there was still very little direct contact between Europeans and Chinese. Goods moved very, very slowly via the Silk Road, and the prospect of goods reaching their destination was precarious at best. But for all intents and purposes, China started opening up to the world. In the example of Zhang Qian, we can see that this was a calculated move coming from the very top, not something haphazard or transitory.

Chapter 19: The Fall of the Han Dynasty

As is the case with any dynasty, the Han dynasty had to finally cease existing at some point. This happened around 220 CE, but the reasons for the downfall of the Han go far back. We find stern criticism of the lack of meritocracy, a crucial prerequisite of the earlier success of the Han, in the works of Xu Gan, an important Confucian who lived in the final years of the Eastern Han dynasty.[93] While praising virtue, Xu Gan noted that times differ and, in certain periods, even the most virtuous men didn't get the praise they deserve. Xu Gan likely felt this way, as he lived during a time when court insidiousness, corruption, and constant strife for influence all reached their peak.

Aware of the roots of the Yellow Turbans and other rebels, Xu Gan saw the good things that came out of the Legalist movement, which was able to bring at least a transitory stability to the Chinese states that had been ravaged by centuries of war during the Warring States Period.

As is so often the case when there are numerous clandestine strivings for power and influence, the emperors turned to people who seemingly didn't belong to any party or clan, such as servants, eunuchs, slaves, etc. One of the last Han Chinese emperors, Ling-ti, relied heavily on his eunuchs when it came to governing his empire. This led to dissatisfaction

---

[93] McLeod, Alexus. "Philosophy in Eastern Han Dynasty China (25-220 CE)." *Philosophy Compass* 10, no. 6 (2015): 355-368.

from the elites, and as was so often the case in ancient (and not so ancient) China, a revolt heated up in the provinces as powerful individuals emerged, wanting to take advantage of the weak central administration.

A very logical conclusion of all this was the so-called Yellow Turban Rebellion, which was motivated by the weak government, natural agrarian disasters, and epidemics. The movement had a strong religious Taoist background and was led by three brothers. Yellow had a special meaning in Taoism, as it signified a new beginning. The movement preached the end of the Han and the coming of a new age, the age of "yellow heaven." The soldiers led by the Chang brothers wore yellow "turbans" or handkerchiefs wrapped around their heads as a way of distinguishing themselves from other groups, hence the name of the whole rebellion.

The Yellow Turbans soon took over a large chunk of the empire, up to two-thirds. The brothers weren't simply involved in religion. They also dabbled in medicine. In the countryside, which had been ravaged by famine, floods, and epidemics, their skills came in handy, allowing them to establish a good relationship with the peasants. To demonstrate how bad it was during this period, let's look at one popular ballad that must have been on every peasant's lips at the time:

"Great chaos in the empire,

The markets were desolate.

Mothers could not protect children,

Wives lost their husbands."[94]

On the other side, in the imperial palace, the emperor wasn't concerned with the growing influence of the Chang brothers, who quickly amassed a following of some 360,000 people by the 180s CE. It is also true that the influence of the Chang brothers reached the imperial palace, and some corrupt eunuchs started, in a way, lobbying in favor of the Yellow Turbans.

The unrest was eventually quenched by the central government around the year 185 CE. But China was already in a very precarious position, with the emergence of powerful warlords who were increasingly

---

[94] Levy, Howard S. "Yellow Turban religion and rebellion at the end of Han." *Journal of the American Oriental Society* 76, no. 4 (1956): 214-227.

thirsty for power. The last Han emperor, Xian, relied heavily on one such warlord, Cao Cao, who was also the chancellor of the empire. Initially, Cao Cao helped the Han dynasty to remain in power, fighting against the Yellow Turbans and other contenders. However, the status of the emperor was by now merely symbolic, and the real power lay in the hands of warlords like Cao Cao or others who managed to get a piece of the Chinese empire.

Cao Cao, like so many before him, possibly tried to unify China once again, but the decisive defeat at the Battle of Red Cliffs restricted his sphere of influence.[95] The Three Kingdoms Period started to emerge after the fall of the Eastern Han, Cao Cao's Wei, as well as Shu-Han and Wu, all led by powerful warlords. It didn't matter that Cao Pi, Cao Cao's son, was declared emperor in 220 CE, the same year when Cao Cao died. The great Han dynasty ceased to exist, as did the unified Chinese state.

There are many reasons for the ascension and downfall of the Eastern Han. It seems the early Eastern Han were able to keep a firm grip over the country, allowing the Chinese people to develop. But as the years passed and the memory of the Western Han's downfall became dimmer, the Eastern Han grew increasingly divorced from what was happening in their empire, caring more about carnal pleasures and their own vanity. By forgetting the big lesson of the Western Han, they were doomed to become another lesson for the next dynasty.

For the next sixty years, up until 280 CE, China would be divided into three spheres of influence until it was once again unified, this time under the Jin dynasty. This marked the end of ancient China and brings us to the end of our journey. However, this is the start of another story, the story of medieval China.

The period of the Three Kingdoms and the period that directly preceded it is remembered by the Chinese people as being fairly tumultuous. Old power hierarchies were abolished, and a window was opened for those who had the wits and courage to take their once-in-a-lifetime opportunity. Cao Cao was one such gentleman, even though he didn't live to see the fully fledged Three Kingdoms period. Cao Cao himself expressed the joys of this unpredictable but exciting period and lifestyle in the following passage:

---

[95] De Crespigny, Rafe. "Man from the Margin: Cao Cao and the Three Kingdoms." (1990).

"The swift steed in old age may rest in his stable,
But he still thinks of a thousand li journey;
When a hero comes to the end of his days,
Strong heart remains the same.
The time of our life and death
Is more than the whim of Heaven;
If a man is in harmony with himself
He may live for long years."[96]

---

[96] Ibid.

Conclusion

Cao Cao once wrote, "The time of our life and death is more than the whim of Heaven." This is true not only for human life but also for the life of nations, empires, and states. The history (and prehistory) of China is more than a set of haphazard circumstances. It's actually a highly intricate weaving of the fabric of time. Numerous threads make the canvas of Chinese history, and they sometimes intertwine and intermingle in unpredictable and almost incoherent ways.

Sometimes, the threads take their own paths, and what emerges isn't a unified picture but a set of smaller pictures whose complexity we sometimes lose due to the sheer distance of events and their microscopic size. But there's a trend in Chinese history, a trend of reunification (or, inversely, reseparation), where separate threads join and once again intertwine to form a much bigger and often more glorious picture.

From the earliest evidence of Chinese cultures, we can see the conflict between these two trends of unification and separation. They are still at work today, and no one involved, probably not even the main actors, knows where the weight of history will shift next.

However, one thing is certain: China will remain a very important global power, something this country most certainly owes to thousands upon thousands of years of continuous development. Ever since the early days of agriculture, which was where we began this book, the Chinese have heralded technological improvements that very early on made it one of the most populous "countries" in the world (we put "countries" in quotes because the concept of a country as we know it today is a fairly recent development and most certainly didn't exist in the early days of agriculture). The Chinese people quickly optimized the production of grain (not only rice), which made food more available to the people. Having learned the basics of effective agriculture, the Chinese people, in a very similar way to the Egyptians and Mesopotamians, mastered landscape planning, shifting the beds of whole rivers, draining areas important for agricultural production, and controlling the immense power of rivers.

The early days of Chinese culture are wrapped in this vaporous mist of constant battles against the power of water and inevitable floods. The Hebrews are not the only ones with a story of a great flood that came and swept the earth. The Chinese have their own version, and people living at the turning point between prehistory and history had to battle their environment much more than we have to today. No one knows how many Chinese cultures were swept away by torrential floods, but according to something that's still closer to legend than historical fact, Yu the Great, the founder of the legendary Xia dynasty, stopped the floods and provided a basis for the development of all subsequent dynasties.

Unfortunately, we're still in the realm of prehistory with the Xia, as the Chinese writing system took a little bit more time to develop. The Shang are still the earliest proven Chinese dynasty. Thanks to their mastery of writing and the ample evidence they left in the form of oracle bones and bronze vessel inscriptions, we learned quite a lot about the Shang and their way of life in the 2nd millennium BCE.

There is one deep truth linked to the Shang and their writing system, which was refined and further propagated in the millennia to come, resulting in the modern-day Chinese characters. The early writing in China was inextricably tied to the ritual world. There was certainly a practical incentive for developing the writing system. As agriculture, trade, and crafts developed, people started amassing goods. Contracts were established to exchange goods, which was made easier with the help of writing. But equally important, if not more so, was the ritual incentive, the implementation of writing in a carefully constructed system of rituals and beliefs. This is important evidence of the interconnection between the rational and the irrational. Much like thoughts wouldn't exist without emotions, rational, logical writing systems wouldn't exist without the world of mystical rituals. Thanks to discoveries related to the Shang, this deep truth shines even brighter.

The Chinese characters soon crossed the borders of China, whether one turned toward the east (Japan, Korea), south (Indochina), north (Mongolia), or west (Xinjiang, Tibet), helping with the transmission of ideas and data and heralding the cultural developments of whole societies. But the Shang didn't simply bequeath a writing system to their successors. They also left beautifully crafted bronze objects, and their craft of metal production and processing was adopted by surrounding cultures, including the Zhou, who took it to another level.

Learning how to produce and process various metals (especially during the Zhou dynasty when the production of iron was mastered), the Chinese launched themselves into the advanced Age of Metal, which was edified by the invention of their own writing system during the Shang dynasty. The Zhou were strong warriors with effective weapons, and they established a sort of feudal system with their subjugated neighbors, granting relative autonomy to regions that were fairly distant from their centers of power but still exerting strong cultural influence. This interplay between the center and the periphery continues to exist in China to this day. The size of China and its population (which was large even during the Zhou dynasty) made direct administration impossible. The Zhou established a system that worked for centuries, but the precarious balance was ultimately lost since their neighbors grew stronger and demanded more autonomy. Eventually, they demanded to be the next leaders.

One of the first known large-scale conflicts in China, the Warring States Period, ensued. The battles were fierce, long, and exhausting, and China plunged into centuries of conflicts over supremacy. Finally, a new dynasty emerged victorious: the Qin. This dynasty is credited with building the first Chinese empire. As we've seen, there were other Chinese dynasties that came before, but most historians don't dub them "empires." This is because the Qin were the first to systematically address the question of directly administering vast Chinese sub-states/provinces. Their solution, autocracy, was often unjust and ruthless, so the Qin didn't last long.

However, in a similar way to what the Romans were (roughly speaking) contemporaneously doing in Europe, the Qin quickly laid foundations—legal, administrative, and ideological—for an efficient empire.[97] The historical pendulum was now at the other extreme of its predictable trajectory. The Qin were determined to crush all rebellion and to once and for all unify China under one strong ruler. But when this strong ruler, the first Chinese emperor (Qin Shi Huangdi), died, a new conflict started, as the historical pendulum shifted back to a period of fragmentation. The people simply didn't want to tolerate a tyrannical government, and it seemed as if China was going to enter another Warring States Period.

Fortunately for the Chinese people, this time, the final victor and the new emperor, Liu Bang, knew how to lay the foundations for an empire that would last. He founded the famous Han dynasty, the first to build a strong, stable, and prosperous Chinese empire.

The Han dynasty inherited the foundations of the Qin and added a special ingredient, Confucianism, one of the most important "philosophical products" of China, the influence of which is still felt today in modern Chinese politics. Confucianism is a philosophy of societal order, harmony, and virtue. Confucius was also fond of ancient customs, traditions, and rituals, which were carefully preserved by later Confucians. Another important thought was altruism, the supreme love of fellow human beings.

Confucianism came into existence much earlier, during the Spring and Autumn Period, which preceded the Warring States Period. By the time of the Qin dynasty, Confucianism had spread throughout the Chinese states, but the Qin decided that this new philosophy was too dangerous for the new precarious Chinese empire. Much like Mao Zedong's regime persecuted intellectuals and was wary of free-thinking, the Qin decided to crush the Confucian school of thought, accepting the much more narrow-minded, stern, and unempathetic Legalist philosophy. It is actually the Legalist thought that laid the foundations for the first Chinese empire, asserting the emperor as an absolute, supreme ruler, almost a deity, and carefully defining one of the earliest Chinese codes of law. Legalism is not a historical coincidence; after years and years of brutal conflicts, someone had to bring an end to the carnage, but to do this, the first emperor had to be the most brutal of all.

---

[97] It has to be said the Romans really started building their empire, in the constitutional sense, by the end of the 1ˢᵗ century BCE, while the Qin came significantly earlier.

The wisdom of Liu Bang and his successors lies not in their total rejection of Legalism and total acceptance of Confucianism but in their careful balance between the two.

The long period of relative stability allowed for exponential cultural developments. The Han dynasty gave us a fairly cheap way to make lots of paper, which would, combined with the later European printing press, help spread education to millions of people. And this was just a single contribution of the Chinese.

The level of organization in the Han empire was unmatched by anything that came before, even on a global scale. The sheer size of the Chinese population and the vast lands put an almost insurmountable challenge in front of Han statesmen. Practically every village had a chief who was appointed by the central government. He was responsible for applying the government's plan on the micro level. Conscription was universal, with a complex system of different sorts of service types. Trade also started to flourish.

During the Han dynasty, a stable connection, known as the Silk Road, was established between China and Europe. In light of the sheer size, cost, and influence of the modern Belt and Road initiative, this first contact between China and Europe and the establishment of initial trade routes gains even more importance. And the exchange between two large cultural spheres, Chinese and European, resulted in mutual benefits back in the day. Today the Western world, Asian, African, and Latin American countries all benefit from their relationship with China.

For thousands and thousands of years, China was one of the strongest countries in the world. Then, faced with the inevitable atavism of the imperial system, the whole country almost crumbled to pieces during the so-called "century of humiliation," which relates to the Opium Wars and the subsequent subjugation of China by European powers. It is at this point that the historical pendulum reached its extreme, as China dissolved into numerous smaller countries led by power-thirsty warlords. This wasn't a singular occurrence. We've seen in this book that the pendular oscillation between two extremes—fragmentation and unification—is more of a pattern than an exception in thousands and thousands of years of Chinese history (and perhaps even prehistory). And much like the Warring States Period was followed by the Qin dynasty and its incredibly stern tendencies, the chaos of the Warlord Era that took place during the last period of the empire early in the 20th

century was followed by the authoritarian regime of Mao Zedong.

And history will continue to repeat itself, surely. The question is only when and how.

Here's another book by Enthralling History that you might like

Free limited time bonus

Stop for a moment. We have a free bonus set up for you. The problem is this: we forget 90% of everything that we read after 7 days. Crazy fact, right? Here's the solution: we've created a printable, 1-page pdf summary for this book that you're reading now. All you have to do to get your free pdf summary is to go to the following website:

https://livetolearn.lpages.co/enthrallinghistory/

Once you do, it will be intuitive. Enjoy, and thank you!

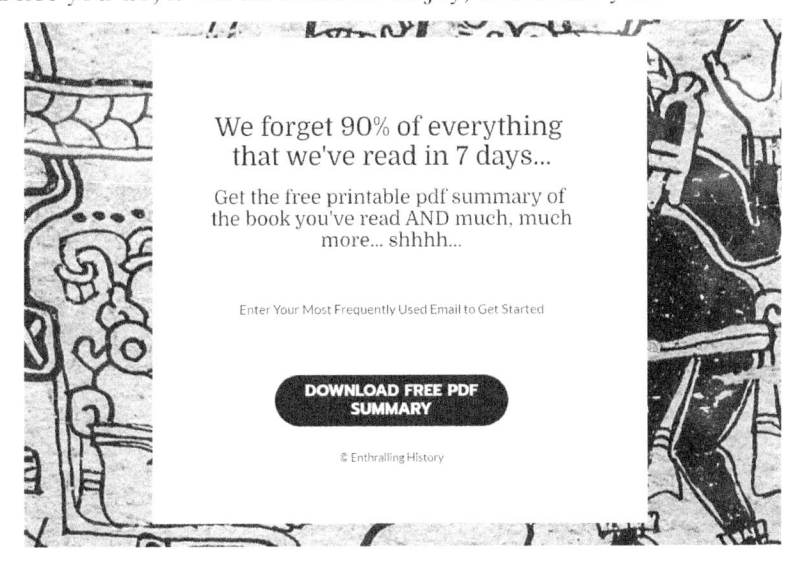

Bibliography

Chang, Kwang-Chih. "In Search of China's Beginnings: New Light on an Old Civilization: A Golden Age of Archaeology is piecing together a new Chinese prehistory and history that differ in fundamental ways from the traditional story." American Scientist 69, no. 2 (1981): 148-160.

Wang, Qian, and Li Sun. "Eightieth year of Peking Man: Current status of Peking Man and the Zhoukoudian site." Anthropological Review 63 (2000): 19-30.

Pu, Li, Chien Fang, Ma Hsing-Hua, Pu Ching-Yu, Hsing Li-Sheng, and Chu Shih-Chiang. "Preliminary study on the age of Yuanmou man by palaeomagnetic technique." Scientia Sinica 20, no. 5 (1977): 645-664.

Boaz, N., and R. Ciochon. "The scavenging of "Peking Man." Natural History 110, no. 2 (2001): 46-51.

Gao, Xing. "Paleolithic cultures in China: uniqueness and divergence." Current Anthropology 54, no. S8 (2013): S358-S370.

Freud, Sigmund. Moses and monotheism. Leonardo Paolo Lovari, 2016.

Yang, Xiaoyan, Zhikun Ma, Jun Li, Jincheng Yu, Chris Stevens, and Yijie Zhuang. "Comparing subsistence strategies in different landscapes of North China 10,000 years ago." The Holocene 25, no. 12 (2015): 1957-1964.

Jing, Yuan. "The origins and development of animal domestication in China." Chinese Archaeology 8, no. 1 (2008): 1-7.

Bestel, Sheahan, Yingjian Bao, Hua Zhong, Xingcan Chen, and Li Liu. "Wild plant use and multi-cropping at the early Neolithic Zhuzhai site in the middle Yellow River region, China." The Holocene 28, no. 2 (2018): 195-207.

Guoping, Sun. "Recent research on the Hemudu culture and the Tianluoshan site." A companion to Chinese archaeology (2013): 555-573.

Wang, Jiajing, Jiangping Zhu, Dongrong Lei, and Leping Jiang. "New evidence for rice harvesting in the early Neolithic Lower Yangtze River, China." Plos one 17, no. 12 (2022): e0278200.

Zhang, Haiwei, Hai Cheng, Ashish Sinha, Christoph Spötl, Yanjun Cai, Bin Liu, Gayatri Kathayat et al. "Collapse of the Liangzhu and other Neolithic cultures in the lower Yangtze region in response to climate change." Science Advances 7, no. 48 (2021): eabi9275.

Ling, Qin. "The Liangzhu culture." A companion to Chinese archaeology (2013): 574-596.

Runnels, Curtis N., Claire Payne, Noam V. Rifkind, Chantel White, Nicholas P. Wolff, and Steven A. LeBlanc. "Warfare in Neolithic Thessaly: A case study." Hesperia: The Journal of the American School of Classical Studies at Athens 78, no. 2 (2009): 165-194.

Liu, Li, Jiajing Wang, Maureece J. Levin, Nasa Sinnott-Armstrong, Hao Zhao, Yanan Zhao, Jing Shao, Nan Di, and Tian'en Zhang. "The origins of specialized pottery and diverse alcohol fermentation techniques in Early Neolithic China." Proceedings of the National Academy of Sciences 116, no. 26 (2019): 12767-12774.

Thorp, Robert L. "Erlitou and the search for the Xia." Early China 16 (1991): 1-38.

Bunker, Emma C. "The Beginning of Metallurgy in Ancient China" Web Archive. Available at: https://web.archive.org/web/20070206143502/http:/exhibits.denverartmuseum.org/asianart/articles/metalwork/art_li_mat.html

Dono, Tsurumatsu. "ON THE COPPER AGE IN ANCIENT CHINA." Bulletin of the Chemical Society of Japan 7, no. 11 (1932): 347-352.

Chen, Minzhen. "Faithful History or Unreliable History: Three Debates on the Historicity of the Xia Dynasty." Journal of Chinese Humanities 5, no. 1 (2019): 78-104.

Allan, Sarah. "The myth of the Xia Dynasty." Journal of the Royal Asiatic Society 116, no. 2 (1984): 242-256.

Mark, Joshua J. "Ancient China." Ancient History Encyclopedia (2012).

Allan, Sarah. ""When Red Pigeons Gathered on Tang's House": A Warring States Period Tale of Shamanic Possession and Building Construction set at the turn of the Xia and Shang Dynasties." Journal of the Royal Asiatic Society 25, no. 3 (2015): 419-438.

Hou, Liangliang, Yaowu Hu, Xinping Zhao, Suting Li, Dong Wei, Yanfeng Hou, Baohua Hu et al. "Human subsistence strategy at Liuzhuang site, Henan, China during the proto-Shang culture (∼ 2000–1600 BC) by stable isotopic analysis." Journal of Archaeological Science 40, no. 5 (2013): 2344-2351.

Guangkuo, Yuan. "The discovery and study of the Early Shang culture." A companion to Chinese archaeology (2013): 323-342.

Shelach, Gideon. "The Qiang and the question of human sacrifice in the late Shang period." Asian Perspectives (1996): 1-26.

Keightley, David N. "Shang divination and metaphysics." Philosophy East and West 38, no. 4 (1988): 367-397.

Qian, Sima. "Records of the Grand Historian of China" Available at: https://archive.org/stream/in.ernet.dli.2015.532974/2015.532974.records-of_djvu.txt

LI, Xiaobing (ed.). "China at War: An Encyclopedia." ABC-CLIO, 2012.

Boltz, William G. "Early Chinese writing." World Archaeology 17, no. 3 (1986): 420-436.

Huang, Chun Chang, Shichao Zhao, Jiangli Pang, Qunying Zhou, Shue Chen, Pinghua Li, Longjiang Mao, and Min Ding. "Climatic aridity and the relocations of the Zhou culture in the southern Loess Plateau of China." Climatic Change 61 (2003): 361-378.

Rawson, Jessica. "Ordering the exotic: ritual practices in the late western and early eastern Zhou." Artibus Asiae 73, no. 1 (2013): 5-76.

Khayutina, Maria. "Western Zhou cultural and historic setting." The Oxford Handbook of Early China (2020): 365.

Childs-Johnson, Elizabeth, ed. The Oxford Handbook of Early China. Oxford University Press, USA, 2020.

Wagner, Donald B. "The earliest use of iron in China." BAR International Series 792 (1999): 1-9.

Cartwright, Mark. Crossbows in Ancient Chinese Warfare. World History Encyclopedia.

Shaughnessy, Edward L. Sources of Western Zhou history: inscribed bronze vessels. Univ of California Press, 1992.

Tu, Wei-Ming. "Confucius and Confucianism." Confucianism and the Family: A Study of Indo-Tibetan Scholasticism (1998): 3-36.

Strickmann, Michel. "History, anthropology, and Chinese religion." (1980): 201-248.

Hsiao, Kung-chuan. "Legalism and autocracy in traditional China." Chinese Studies in History 10, no. 1-2 (1976): 125-143.

Tzu, Sun. The Art of War. Available at: https://sites.ualberta.ca/~enoch/Readings/The_Art_Of_War.pdf

Cartwright, Mark. Warring States Period. World History. Available at: https://www.worldhistory.org/Warring_States_Period/

Fiskesjö, Magnus. "Terra-cotta conquest: The first emperor's clay army's blockbuster tour of the world." Verge: Studies in Global Asias 1, no. 1 (2015): 162-183.

Britannica. Meng Tian. Available at: https://www.britannica.com/biography/Meng-Tian

Kulmar, Tarmo. "On the nature of the governing system of the Qin Empire in ancient China." Folklore: Electronic Journal of Folklore 59 (2014): 165-178.

Guo, Yanzi. "Contingency and Historical Inevitability in the Development of the Qin Dynasty." Journal of Education, Humanities and Social Sciences 8 (2023): 1367-1372.

Zhou, Minhwa, and Meihwa Zhou. "Wisdom and Strategy— An Example for Zhang Liang and Liu Bang." In 7th International Conference on Humanities and Social Science Research (ICHSSR 2021), pp. 941-943. Atlantis Press, 2021.

Chen, Pauline. "History Lessons." New York Times, 1993.

Hardy, Grant, and Anne Behnke Kinney. The establishment of the Han empire and imperial China. Greenwood Publishing Group, 2005.

Cullen, Christopher. "Motivations for scientific change in ancient China: Emperor Wu and the Grand Inception astronomical reforms of 104 BC." Journal for the History of Astronomy 24, no. 3 (1993): 185-203.

Dreyer, Edward L. "Zhao Chongguo: A Professional Soldier of China's Former Han Dynasty." The Journal of Military History 72, no. 3 (2008): 665-725.

Gao, Jiyi. "Emperor Xuan, Emperor Zhang and the Rise and Decline of Zhangju in the Han Dynasty." Hanxue Yanjiu (Chinese Studies) 25, no. 1 (2007).

Xiong, Victor Cunrui, and Kenneth James Hammond, eds. Routledge Handbook of Imperial Chinese History. Routledge, 2019. p. 25-38.

L'Haridon, Béatrice. "WANG MANG 王莽 (c. 45 BCE-23 CE) AND CLASSICAL LEARNING AS PATH TO SUPREME POWER." Early China 45 (2022): 51-72.

Dubs, Homer H. "The victory of Han Confucianism." Journal of the American Oriental Society 58, no. 3 (1938): 435-449.

Xueqin, Li, and Xing Wen. "New light on the Early-Han code: a reappraisal of the Zhangjiashan bamboo-slip legal texts." Asia Major (2001): 125-146.

Hardy, Grant, and Anne Behnke Kinney. The establishment of the Han empire and imperial China. Greenwood Publishing Group, 2005.

Bottéro, Françoise, and Christoph Harbsmeier. "The Shuowen Jiezi Dictionary and the Human Sciences in China." Asia Major (2008): 249-271.

Nylan, Michael. "Sima Qian: A True Historian?" Early China 23 (1998): 203-246.

Cartwright, Mark. Paper in ancient China. World history encyclopedia, 2017.

Zhijie, Huo. "The significance of female education during the Han Dynasty." Вестник Бурятского государственного университета. Гуманитарные исследования Внутренней Азии 4 (2016): 54-59.

Van Ess, Hans. "Emperor Wu of the Han and the First August Emperor of Qin in Sima Qian's Shiji." Birth of an Empire 5 (2013): 239.

Ch'ien, Mu. Merits and Demerits of Political Systems in Dynastic China. Springer Berlin Heidelberg, 2019.

Juping, Yang. "The Relations between China and India and the Opening of the Southern Silk Road during the Han Dynasty." The Silk Road 11 (2013): 82-92.

McLeod, Alexus. "Philosophy in Eastern Han Dynasty China (25–220 CE)." Philosophy Compass 10, no. 6 (2015): 355-368.

Levy, Howard S. "Yellow Turban religion and rebellion at the end of Han." Journal of the American Oriental Society 76, no. 4 (1956): 214-227.

De Crespigny, Rafe. "Man from the Margin: Cao Cao and the Three Kingdoms." (1990).

Printed in Great Britain
by Amazon